SUV Madness

a short history

John Everett

Grosvenor House
Publishing Limited

This book is published by
Grosvenor House Publishing Ltd
Link House
140 The Broadway, Tolworth, Surrey, KT6 7HT.
www.grosvenorhousepublishing.co.uk

A CIP record for this book
is available from the British Library

ISBN 978-1-83975-305-3

*"I would like to acknowledge my thanks to Becky Banning
from Grosvenor House. Her support has been absolutely
wonderful and, in many ways, I am indebted to her for
managing to get this book into its final completed form.*

Thank you, Becky!"

Dedicated to my wonderful wife, Jeanne, who shames me with her determination to keep her precious seventeen-year-old VW Polo on the road to the bitter end.

Also to my children and their families. Each of them, in their own different ways, inspire me to become a better, stronger person.

Chapter Index

TABLE INDEX

ABOUT THE AUTHOR

John lives in Durham with his wife Jeanne, to whom he has been married for 38 years. They have three children with their own families and children.

John studied economics and sociology at the University of Kent and spent three years doing part-time post-graduate research at the University of Warwick. In 1986 he moved with his family to Durham, where he began training for ordination in the Church of England. He decided, however, that his vocation wasn't in the priesthood and then spent many years working in building management, latterly at Durham University. More recently, he has had various professional roles promoting wind power, one of them as a director of Green Campaigns Ltd. For a number of years he was an active Greenpeace member. He is indebted to them and other campaigning organizations such as Friends of the Earth, WWF and the RSPB for their contribution to his environmental awareness.

John has written extensively throughout his adult life on a range of subjects, including the content for a number of websites which he has created and administered. Two book-length critiques, written to expose the methods of a radical Christian community, have enjoyed wide circulation despite not having been published in a traditional format.

John is enthusiastic about animal welfare and environmental protection. He spends an increasing amount of time birdwatching, gardening, wildflower-identifying, and generally enjoying both rural and urban nature. He considers himself to be one of Luton Town FC's most passionate supporters: with Jeanne, he travels considerable distances to watch them play. Having been genuinely passionate, too, about running, his achievements include finishing 20 Great North Runs; one of them in 90 minutes. Sadly, he had to hang up his running boots in 2019, and his walking boots are currently stored away due to complications following knee-replacement surgery. Reading widely, playing piano and listening to music, concert-going, camping-van and canvass camping, as well as watching movies and a wide variety of TV, are other interests that have largely – but not entirely – helped keep him out of mischief; and they still do.

PREFACE

July 2nd. 2020

It's better to light a candle than curse the darkness

Ancient Chinese motto used by Amnesty International

SUV Madness is a treatise born from frustration; frustration at finding myself increasingly surrounded by vehicles which enrage me as surely as the proverbial red rag would do if I were a bull. Their ubiquity upsets me, and I'm constantly being unsettled by noticing so many of them when I'm out and about – which isn't really a very healthy way to live.

Rather than simply howl at the moon or rage against the machine, I decided to commit my thoughts to paper; a process which has been extremely educational at the same time. But what I had originally supposed would be a lengthy analytical discussion has morphed into a small book. As such, it may not be so accessible to the casual reader as I'd originally hoped. Despite the book being short, I'm aware that it will take a certain commitment from the reader, and I suspect that most of those willing to make such a commitment will be those who already dislike SUVs before they've even read the first page. To broaden its interest, therefore, I've also offered something of myself by way of storytelling. Those who see the book through to the end will not only know more about the impact of SUVs on the environment, they will also know something about me; something about who I am and what makes me tick. My hope – and I trust it's not a conceited one – is that this will soften the book's potential polemic and invigorate the terrible tedium of statistical analysis, thereby making it an engaging read for all alike.

I would like to explain that I'm not an out-and-out, powerful-vehicle Luddite who can't appreciate engineering excellence. For better or worse, I've been fascinated since childhood by the technology of transport: planes, trams, trains, buses, lorries, and, indeed, cars. And, being an ardent fan of most sports, I've been glued to the TV screen for many an F1 Grand Prix. The final lap of the final race of the 2008 F1 season had my heart pounding just as intensely as the deciding over of the 2019 cricket world cup did: both were genuinely remarkable, once-in-a-lifetime events which appeared to be beyond belief. It will be hard to forget Martin Brundle's Brazilian Grand Prix commentary as he called out that Lewis Hamilton had overtaken Timo Glock's stricken Toyota on the final rain-soaked corner to snatch the championship from Felipe Massa, who had already punched a celebratory fist in the air when he took the chequered flag. What amazing drama!

Skeletons like this in my make-the-world-a-better-place credibility cupboard will, in eyes of some, disqualify me from being considered authentic even though I no longer enjoy F1 racing in the way I once did. Truth be told, I haven't watched a Grand Prix for many years; but it hasn't been a conscious choice not to, it's just that other things seem to have filled that particular space in my leisure time. In the light of the conclusions which my research have led me to, however, my abstention may well now become a matter of principle to boot.

My issue with SUVs is largely an issue with the harm they cause, and this book discusses the damage done by the recent explosion in ownership. I will argue that ignorance of the damage is no excuse for it: too many are culpably unwilling to link the SUV *cause* with the environmental *effect*. If I want others to start making the necessary connections and take action, then I should do the same myself. So my days of watching conventional F1 motor racing are surely numbered; but can electric-powered Formula E racing come to my rescue? I've not yet had the opportunity to look into it or get involved as a spectator, although I've noticed that Greenpeace have given it the thumbs up and their wonderful animatronic polar bear has been photographed trackside, so that looks like a promising endorsement. Similarly, electric-powered road cars may well prove to be something of an environmental salvation for those who simply can't kick the SUV habit: a number of manufacturers already have electric SUVs on the market, and there are many more in the manufacturing pipeline. If these vehicles are indeed going to help in the fight to control global warming, and there are some important "ifs" which I shall discuss, then due thanks will need to be given to the role which wind power has played as a renewable source of electrical energy. And with that said, I think I know the subject for my next writing project. It will be one which tells a story of equal vigour to the one told here.

There is no missionary motive in what I've written. I've little doubt that SUVs are here to stay, and the sales' surge of petrol and diesel models still has considerable room to run before they are phased out by legislation in favour of electric models. A few automotive commentators have even suggested that at some not-too-distant point the SUV design will have become more or less synonymous with what we think of as a car. Maybe that's taking things too far, or maybe not. Whatever the case may be, I don't have any illusions about their remaining popular for the foreseeable future, and nothing I can say will make the slightest difference. What I would therefore ask my reader to bear in mind is that my main objective is to provide hard evidence of the scale to which SUV ownership has jeopardized UK attempts to control car emissions. As such, it will underscore my concern that there is a large segment of the population whose willingness to make the lifestyle changes necessary to bring climate change under control is questionable, to say the least. I will be suggesting that owning an SUV, especially one of the larger models, is a careless and callous poke in the eye to environmental welfare. I may not be able to change behaviour, but I can at least do my bit to ensure that the eco-vandalism of SUV-buying madness is called out for what it is.

PREFACE POST-SCRIPT

July 24th

When I began my research in March this year, the crucial Department for Transport (DfT) table VEH0160 had been updated to Q3 of 2019. I made frequent checks, but no updated information had been made available by the time I finished my initial data analysis and first draft 'SUV madness' itself. This meant that the last full year for which I had complete data – Q1 to Q4 – was 2018. By the time I'd begun to scrutinize in fine detail what I'd written, however, the DfT table had been updated to Q1 of 2020, which made 2019 the most recent complete year. I have re-analysed the updated information and incorporated it into the text in all of the places where this was necessary, and also – so far as possible – where it was practical. In the instances where I have retained 2018 for full-year data analysis, in tables 1 and 2 for example, there is no essential conflict with the arguments or explanations of my discussion.

CHAPTER ONE

SUPER SEXY SUVs

In February 2020, when I first began my research, the coronavirus threat was still a distant one; little more than a small dark cloud on the horizon. We worried about it, yet we still hoped it would pass us by – and many of us expected it to. We all know, however, how quickly those small, puffy, cumulus clouds can multiply to obliterate the sun entirely and ruin what had promised to be a glorious day. The change to our lifestyles during those comparatively short springtime weeks managed to temporarily knock the great god of economic expansion off its complacent throne: even the welfare of gross domestic product had to begin playing second fiddle to the greater good of the nation's health and the ability of our medical services to cope with an unprecedented global pandemic. Perhaps the realignment of what we consider to be important will survive beyond the turning tide of state lockdowns. Perhaps many of us will find ourselves refreshed by having had to make do with less of everything and the discovery that doing so is no bad thing after all. Who can tell what life is going to be like *on the other side*?

This is something of a strange way to introduce a discussion about the rise and rise of SUVs in our modern world. But who knows what changes to the economic order will result from the restrictions imposed on us as we tried, collectively, to prevent ourselves from being overwhelmed by a plague of innumerable, microscopic, Covid-19 viral parasites. The choices we were making about our vehicles of preference when I began my research may no longer be the choices of the future. If not, then I for one will welcome any changes which genuinely benefit the environment. We may, in fact, have no *choice* other than to change the way we live now: car factories all across the world have been closing as, temporarily at least, demand has collapsed and as the welfare of workers has needed to take precedence over all other considerations. The nature of post-pandemic car-buying demand may well be hugely different to what it has been in the recent past, as will be the ability of the industry to meet that demand: which carmakers survive remains to be seen. The SUV story told in this small book, therefore, might well be considered historical: a story of how things were before the world changed; a story with an ending that remains to be written by the events of the coming years and which may well be very different to the one I would have predicted when I began writing it. On the other hand, the international love affair with SUVs – and the UK's one in particular – may have simply been put on hold for a few months. Sadly, I think this is the most likely scenario, but time will tell.

The motivation which enabled me to spend literally days and weeks organising and analysing GB car registration statistics was predicated on a rather negative emotion: a sense that, together, we have little chance of success in the fight against climate change given that our lifestyle choices are so deeply influenced by the "my" culture: *my* right to take cheap flights; *my* right to eat cheap meat; and, perversely, *my* right to buy any car I like, even a comparatively expensive one. When I read an article by the environmental charity, Hubbub, and discovered that almost half of the flights taken in 2019 by British men aged between 20 and 45 were for stag-dos, and 35% of those taken by women in the same age group were for hen parties, it simply reinforced my conviction that the effort of *some* to curb their air miles is going to be little more than tokenism given the wanton carelessness of the *many*.

Similarly, looking around most supermarkets and seeing the outrageous quantity of cheap chicken on sale makes me feel something like that tormented person in the famous Edvard Munch painting: I feel as though I'd like to clasp both hands to the side of my horrified face and let out a primal scream right there and then in the aisles; so too when I see the long, snaking, bumper-to-bumper queues at KFC drive-throughs. It's not just thinking about the conditions that these wretched creatures are kept in – or should I say manufactured in? – which turns my stomach, it's also the inability of many to join up the dots and make the association between cheap meat and rainforest destruction. Incomprehensibly large tracts of forest are cleared each year and replaced with mile-after-mile of monoculture soybean plantations; soya being one of the primary foods used to fatten up all those billions of hapless factory-farmed chickens across the world. Thanks to the efforts of international environmental organisations and domestic opposition (especially from indigenous populations), the Amazon rainforest is one that has enjoyed some protection in recent years from soya-driven clearance; but the ruthless soybean industry has simply turned its attention to other parts of Brazil such as the savannahs and forests of the Cerrado. Meanwhile, massive Amazonian logging operations are being sanctioned by Brazil's maverick president, and the cleared expanses are now used for cattle grazing. It's very much a case of *out of the chicken-feed pot and into the cattle-meat fire*. Rainforest clearance operations aren't just bad news for the endangered animals whose habitats are destroyed, they are also bad news for the climate as the world is left with fewer and fewer trees to capture and store the increasing amounts of carbon being generated. The dots are easy enough to join up for those who wish to do so; but I fear that many don't.

That many don't, or won't, join up the dots of the cheap-meat production trail was well illustrated by the queues at our local KFC fast food restaurant when lockdown restrictions began easing back in June. If I'd thought the queues were bad enough in the past, they were eclipsed tenfold by those made up of people who were prepared to wait an hour or more to get their KFC fix: queues in excess of fifty cars backed up in a serpentine trail around the retail centre car park and out onto the road. I'm well aware that Hugh Fernley-Wittingstall must have given a measure of acceptability to KFC chicken by tweeting his support for the company's decision to sign up to the "European Chicken

Commitment", a set of requirements drawn up by a coalition of animal protection groups.[1] But isn't this sign-up decision little more than a confession to the historic and ongoing cruelty inflicted on all those countless millions of birds which, for decades, have ended up as battered nuggets in a KFC carton? A spokesperson for the company replied to Fernley-Wittingstall's tweet saying he was delighted to be starting the journey of improved animal welfare – a very long journey through to 2026. The flip side to this was surely an implicit admission that the way chickens are currently treated, and have been all along, is cruel. And perhaps of even more importance is the admission that welfare of these chickens and the way they are treated actually matters. So why haven't KFC done anything before? And why do so many people tacitly support the barbaric way in which the chickens are treated by not only giving KFC their custom but also flocking in their droves to do so? I can only think that the avuncular face of Colonel Sanders grinning at them from thousands of signs across the country has induced some kind of hypnotic amnesia to the cruelty behind it all. If the KFC queues are reflective of what it is the British public crave, then the signs for any lasting improvement on the way we behave – which some felt might be a mitigatory outcome of the pandemic – aren't good ones.

I find it hard to imagine how we shall ever successfully tackle the climate emergency when selfish consumerism, together with denial and head-burying, has such a stranglehold over the way we live. Does that make me a pessimistic defeatist? I hope not! I'd prefer to think that I'm just facing up to facts, being a realist if you like. I say that cautiously as I'm well aware that many who like to think themselves plain-talking, many who tell you they always say it like it is, those who fearlessly speak truth to power and champion the need to drain the swamps of corruption; these same people can be infected with a hubris which makes them feel superior to lesser mortals, to those who can't see things the way they really are or

---

[1] Twitter comment from Hugh Fearnley-Wittingstall. July 12th. 2019: https://twitter.com/hughfw/status/1149597736288735233?lang=en

are too faint hearted to speak out if they do. I very much hope I'm not someone who takes self-deceptive pride in their realism, and I try to guard against becoming such a person. Even so, I still like to believe that my negative assessment of the way things are makes me more of a pragmatist than a pessimist: I don't go about with wild eyes like Private Fraser in "Dad's Army" dejectedly announcing that *we're all doomed*; and, like Wilkins Micawber from "David Copperfield", I retain a hope that against all odds *something will come up*. That *something*, however, will need to be powerful enough to perform the kind of miracle King Canute was unable to: it will need to turn back the incoming tide of unthinking acquisitive avarice which is blind to the command of most outstretched hands, even those of a king. Simon Kuper of the Financial Times is clearly of the same mind, as evidenced by the conclusions he came to in an article entitled, "The Myth of Green Growth". He asks the question: *Can democracy survive without carbon?*[1] And his basic answer is that we're not going to have the chance to find out!

Set within the context of continued global increases in annual CO_2 emissions, Kuper's article provides an assessment of what needs to happen in order to avoid a climate catastrophe. And given the Intergovernmental Panel on Climate Change's warning that we'll need to almost halve global CO_2 emissions by 2030 in order to keep temperature increases below the requisite 1.5°, he lists some of the drastic measures which he envisages will be required straight away:

stop most flying, meat-eating and clothes-buying until we have green alternatives, ban privately owned cars and abandon sprawling suburbs.

---

[1] The Financial Times: "The myth of green growth": www.ft.com/content/47b0917c-f523-11e9-a79c-bc9acae3b654

Drastic changes like this, he argues, are the ones required given the magnitude of the problem. But he doesn't have any confidence they will happen:

*No electorate will vote to decimate its own lifestyle. We can't blame bad politicians or corporates. **It's us: we will always choose growth over climate.*** (My emphasis)

If my concern about the runaway demand for cheap flights and cheap meat across much of the world leads me to agree with Kuper and conclude there is little hope of averting the climate apocalypse, then these fears are further reinforced by having had to witness the extraordinary increase on our roads of a type of car which has become my bête noire: the SUV; the Sport Utility Vehicle; the grown-ups' Tonka toy with big wheels and rugged features; the plaything of the urban vain; the status-statement of those who've made it, think they've made it or want others to think they've made it! If that sounds rather broad-brush and unfair, then I shall put things right by offering some more nuanced definitions as we proceed. But when even Jaguar Land Rover acknowledges that the new range of the iconic Defender has been designed with *on-road* as much as *off-road* use in mind, then perhaps my cynicism can at least be understood. It's purely by coincidence that I happened to be writing this chapter at the same time as car magazines released their reviews of the Defender 90 and 110 models, which are due to start being delivered this summer.

The new Land Rover Defender. Photo from shutterstock.com under licence

I predict that by Spring 2021, in spite of the Covid-19 pandemic and a *starting* price tag of about £41,000, the new Defenders will have become an increasingly common sight on our streets; starting in London and working outwards – just like the virus. Farmers probably won't be buying many until the cheaper, "commercial" version becomes available. Autocar magazine has quoted Nick Rogers, executive director of product engineering for Land Rover, as saying:

It is not only the most capable Land Rover ever, but also a truly comfortable, modern vehicle that people will love to drive.[1]

The article also informs us about Land Rover's future plans:

Leaked details suggest that Land Rover's plans to keep updating the Defender family are already well advanced, with a larger 130 model said to be being prepped for a launch in 2022. An internal

---

[1] Autocar website. Car news page. "New Land Rover Defender – UK prices confirmed for 90 and 110": www.autocar.co.uk/car-news/new-cars/new-land-rover-defender-2019

document published online has described the car as a "Premium explorer" for "families, active lifestyle and travel".

And...

In contrast, an ultra-capable off-roader is said to be only at the consideration stage, as the base car is believed to have more capability than almost any buyer could require.

Jaguar Land Rover clearly has its eyes on the luxury, high-end of the market; the end already well served by SUVs such as the BMW X5 and Mercedes G-Wagens. The new Defender isn't a vehicle which farmers are going to risk getting battered about in the way the old ones were, and still are. As someone, like most, with more than a soft spot for the old Defender, it sticks in my gullet to say it...but this is just what we *don't* need right now when facing a climate emergency. Consider this: there will initially be a choice of 4 or 6-cylinder petrol and diesel engines available; across the range, the CO_2 emissions will vary from 230 to 255 g/km and the fuel efficiency will vary from 25.2 to 32.2 mpg.[1] I shall be exploring the environmental impact of high CO_2 emissions and poor fuel efficiency in some detail in following chapters, so suffice for now to say that European vehicle legislation[2] requires Jaguar Land Rover as a group to have a fleet average of no more than 135 g/km on new car sales in 2020.[3] The addition of the new Defender to the company's fleet range will inevitably make it harder to meet the target and avoid heavy fines. I haven't been able to find out how the company intends to comply. Maybe there will be some kind of

[1] BBC Top Gear website. Reviews: www.topgear.com/car-reviews/land-rover/defender-1/owning

[2] The legislation requires manufacturers to ensure that, during 2020, 95% of new "fleet" sales are comprised of vehicles which result in an average of 95 grams of CO_2 per kilometer or less. Each "group" of manufacturers, however, have been allotted specific targets based on sale volumes and average vehicle size.

[3] Autocar magazine website. Car news page. "Analysis – How will car makers meet new CO_2 laws?" Hilton Holloway: www.autocar.co.uk/car-news/industry/analysis-how-will-car-makers-meet-new-co2-laws

fudge? Given these compliance challenges, it makes you wonder how the group's production chiefs can feel confident enough to launch a new model range with such an outrageous carbon footprint. It's down to consumer demand, of course. If the public wants something badly enough, then manufacturers will find a way to supply it so they can make a handsome profit.

As in the case of chicken consumption, so too with SUV purchases: many just don't care or haven't thought it all through well enough. So, once again, it's the inability of the many to join up the trail of those flaming tell-tale dots which causes me such dismay. And for someone with a visceral hatred of these outsized vehicles, it's been extremely testing having had to stand by and watch their numbers increase at what, to me, has seemed to be an alarming rate. My woke environmental sensibilities have trained me to think of "SUV" as a kind of dirty word; a swear word that shouldn't be used in polite company and only ever acceptable when no other word is available. There seems to be no social shame for most, however, in using the word without any sense of the need to then apologize for having done so. Car advertisers are proud to use SUV as an allurement to potential buyers: *our* latest SUV is better than *their* SUV. Moving with the times, no one in the UK car industry is any longer snooty about SUVs; and no one seems to think there is anything undignified about owning one, nothing a bit gross or American. The badge of SUV ownership is one which many now aspire to wear, and car manufacturers are falling over one another in the rush to give the public what the public wants. Even that stalwart of British engineering excellence, Aston Martin, has fallen under the spell and begun dancing to the piped tune of customer demand. In November 2019 it was announced that the Aston Martin DBX SUV will go on sale in the UK from £158,000. A review on the EVObsession website (EV = Electric Vehicle) eagerly announced that a hybrid model is to be included in the range and will be fitted with a Mercedes' turbo straight-six: [1]

That's right. The same 429 HP straight-six that's coupled with an electric motor, a twin-scroll turbo, and an electric compressor in the AMG E53 super sedan is being prepped for duty in Aston Martin's super-sexy SUV.[2]

There! My very worst fears confirmed in a sentence: the Aston Martin DBX is not just sexy, it's *super-sexy*. What, may I ask, is sexy about *any* car? I recognize that the adjective is widely abused and has had its meaning blurred by incongruous juxtapositions with all kinds of nouns such as *smartphone*, but I'm rather afraid that some people really *do* think that there's something sexy about, say, the shape of a Range Rover Evoque? No doubt their drivers are hopeful that some of the sexiness will rub off onto them. Sadly, I think that in the eyes of some it does. For those wealthy people who are attracted to the Aston Martin DBX but are worried about the environmental credentials of the model shown off to the press (a model fitted with, to quote from Autocar magazine, *a Mercedes-derived 4.0 litre, twin-turbocharged V8 engine that produces some 550 Hp and more than 500 lb-ft of torque*), buying the mild-hybrid model should allow them to sleep easily at night according to the logic of Mojojojo Barras's EVObsession review. But perhaps they *shouldn't* sleep easily. In fact, they *definitely* shouldn't! The Mercedes-AMG E53 sedan fitted with exactly the same mild-hybrid engine only manages to

---

[1] Hybrid vehicles, or hybrid electric vehicles, use battery-powered motors together with their petrol/diesel engines. The batteries themselves are charged through the vehicles' own engine power. The electric motors in mild-hybrid vehicles (MHEVs) only *assist* the main engine, whereas the electric motors of full-hybrid vehicles (HEVs) are capable of powering the cars on their own for a short distance.

[2] EVObsession website. "First-ever Aston Martin SUV will be available as a hybrid." Mojojojo Barras: https://evobsession.com/first-ever-aston-martin-suv-will-be-available-as-a-hybrid-20-pics/

achieve a meagre 23 mpg on a combined cycle[1] and has somewhat staggering CO_2 emissions of 289 g/km – an "average" SUV emits 143 g/km, but more of that later.

Lat me back-peddle for just a moment and go into confessional mode. Whilst trying to make sure I had at least some idea what I was talking about with regard to car engines, I visited the official Mercedes-Benz website to gen up on the AMG 4.0-litre V8 biturbo engine; one of those which will be fitted in *non-hybrid* Aston Martin DBX SUVs (biturbo is shorthand for twin-turbo). Do, please, take a look.[2] The word *turbo* is another one that has been abused by association with entirely inappropriate things such as the maximum setting on an electric ceiling fan. A turbo – short for turbocharger – is actually a mechanical device which is fitted into an internal combustion engine. It utilizes exhaust fumes to generate extra compressed air which is then forced into the combustion chamber, thereby increasing the engine's ignition power. On many car engines it is fitted externally; but on the afore-mentioned V-formation AMG engine the twin turbos are fitted internally in what Mercedes describe as a "hot inside V". Simply looking at pictures of the engine, I found myself very nearly transfixed with the same incredulous admiration I've always had for all kinds of different machines which represent the very height of engineering precision and excellence. I could even have been tempted to use the word "sexy" if I hadn't known better. An engine like this is almost beyond belief; it is quintessentially superb: there isn't really any other way to describe it. Sadly, this doesn't justify its deployment in a vehicle to be driven on British roads, or *any* surface that isn't a racetrack. The relationship between technology and its use in a social context is a fascinating subject of industrial ethics which many sociologists have written about in depth. It's not possible for

---

[1] Carbuzz website. "2020 Mercedes-AMG E53 4matic": https://carbuzz.com/cars/mercedes-benz/amg-e53-coupe/2020-mercedes-amg-e53-4matic-coupe
[2] Mercedes-Benz website. "The new AMG 4.0-litre V8 biturbo engine": www.mercedes-benz.com/en/innovation/vehicle-development/the-new-amg-4-0-litre-v8-biturbo-engine

me, however, to do any more than make some superficial observations. I have no underlying issue with the actual hardware of SUVs or their engines, taken in isolation. But it's almost impossible to disentangle a piece of machinery, or any artefact for that matter, from the social framework in which it's manufactured and used. This is well illustrated when we consider the atrocious sweat-shop conditions that make the manufacture of mass-produced supermarket clothing possible. All too often we switch off, possibly as a defence mechanism against becoming overwhelmed; and we end up spending our money on things we really oughtn't to. SUVs are no exception, and manufacturers are only too happy to design and produce the very finest machines that we, the general public, are able and willing to pay for.

It's not just Aston Martin, *most* of the luxury-vehicle manufacturers are in on the act: Jaguar has the E-Pace, F-Pace and all-electric I-Pace; Rolls Royce has the Cullinan V12, and Porsche has the Macan and the Cayenne. Of the 12,489 Porsche vehicles which were registered in Great Britain during 2018, more than half – 6,282 – were SUVs. And these gargantuan cars haven't just received the thumbs up from the wealthy: car magazine reviewers – a hard bunch to please – have also waxed lyrical about their superiority. Here's an extract from the Motor1.com review of the Cayenne Turbo S E-hybrid, written by Greg Fink. It could almost have been written as a parody on car reviews; but it's one-hundred percent kosher:

The 2020 Porsche Cayenne Turbo S E-hybrid follows a simple recipe: take one part Cayenne Turbo, another part Cayenne E-Hybrid, and stir. The resulting dish is a monstrous concoction... even Dr. Frankenstein might think the Turbo S E-Hybrid is a bit much.

Predictably, the Turbo S E-Hybrid is an absolutely savage instrument in a straight line and its 683 pound-feet of torque provide a brutal kick in the gut with each and every launch-control-induced acceleration run. Despite the all-wheel-drive crossover's sticky Pirelli tyres momentarily slipping at takeoff, the top-of-the-line Cayenne rockets to 60 mph in a manufacturer-estimated 3.6 seconds.[1]

If I'd not known better, I could easily have thought that Fink was reviewing a jet-propelled vehicle designed to make an attempt at the land speed record.

Bentley entered the SUV market with its Bentayga model in 2015. And, in September 2019, the company's online newsroom announced the arrival of a plug-in hybrid electric version:

Bentley has announced that the pioneering Bentayga Hybrid – the luxury SUV sector's first true plug-in hybrid – is now on sale in Europe. Handcrafted in Crewe, England, the latest version of Bentley's exquisitely appointed SUV will be the company's most efficient model ever, with CO_2 emissions of just 79 g/km (WLTP – weighted, combined).

The Bentayga Hybrid is the ultimate grand tourer, offering a serene and luxurious driving experience through future-focussed technology.[2]

The WLTP (Worldwide Harmonised Light Vehicle Test Procedure) is intended to give an emissions rating for vehicles that is based on "realistic" driving conditions in the new world of electrified vehicles. So it would appear that this new Bentley, with its extremely modest emissions rating of 79 g/km, is something of a breakthrough in the world of luxury-vehicle "green" driving.

---

[1] Motor1.com website. "2020 Porsche Cayenne Turbo S E-Hybrid first drive: Electrification intensification": https://uk.motor1.com/reviews/364761/2020-porsche-cayenne-turbo-se-hybrid-first-drive/
[2] Bentley Newsroom. "Bentley's first step towards electrification – the Bentayga hybrid": www.bentleymedia.com/en/newsitem/999-bentleys-first-step-towards-electrification-the-bentayga-hybrid

Given, however, that the pure-electric range is only just over 24 miles, the *real* realistic data for the vehicle is likely to be considerably higher if it is often taken for longer journeys on the open road beyond the city; and I assume many of them will be. I shall return to this issue in chapter seven when I discuss electric vehicles.

An SUV madness seems to have fallen on every sector of British society, a madness that has also attained pandemic proportions within Western society in general. It's one of the main reasons why I can't feel optimistic about our collective effort to contain global warming. I don't imagine I'm alone in thinking like this, but very little statistical analysis seems be available about "the SUV problem", as I dare to call it. So, in order to do something more than simply throw stones and hand out insults, I decided to take a more in-depth look for myself. It was the beginning of something of a pilgrimage and my findings will unfold as we progress through the following chapters.

At the heart of my research is Department for Transport table VEH0160[1] of vehicle registrations. I downloaded and analysed this huge spreadsheet to obtain reliable and comprehensive statistics about national car sales. Having done so, I soon found myself caught between a rock and a hard place with respect to the presentation of my conclusions. On the one hand I wanted to write with at least a measure of academic credibility, but on the other I wanted to ensure that my discussion remained accessible, engaging and personal. Squaring the circle in this respect is almost impossible: statistics, ultimately, are statistics, and they cannot be sexed-up very much, however hard one tries. But so far as possible I've consigned the finer detail of my analytical assumptions and mathematics to the appendices, and I've pointed to these where necessary in the footnotes. The distinction between "registrations" and "sales", for example, is made clear in Appendix one, as is the

---

[1] Gov.uk website. All vehicles page. Vehicles registered for the first time by make and model: www.gov.uk/government/collections/vehicles-statistics

distinction between data applying to either GB or the UK. If any aspect of the arguments which I make in the main chapters of my discussion appears to be wrong, I would urge my readers to review the appendices before concluding that I'm mistaken. If any aspect of my arguments seems confusing, then the appendices might similarly be helpful; otherwise, I would suggest reading on until all – hopefully – becomes clear.

CHAPTER TWO

INTRODUCING THE SUV PROBLEM

Why do I consider the growth of SUV ownership to be a problem? I'll come clean and admit that I hadn't given it too much thought until sometime during 2007 I watched a Greenpeace video which mocked ownership of oversized off-road vehicles for domestic and social use.[1] The video was a jaunty little thing, made as a TV commercial with pacey, foot-tapping, drive-along music to underpin the action. It showed a day in the office life of a casual, smart-looking young man who radiated self-confidence. Behind his back, however, he was constantly being mocked by the other office staff; and although a cheeky-looking girl had a charming smile on her face when she gave him a cup of coffee, we viewers knew that she'd previously spat into the cup: *properly* spat a considerable amount of spittle into it. At the end of the office day he casually picks up his jacket and flicks his car keys up with a man-about-town nonchalance. Having cheerily said goodbye to his colleagues, he gets into the lift. We see, then, that the words "I am a prick" have been attached to the back of his jacket. And as he drives his 4x4 out of the car park, we also see that someone has written "wanker" on the dusty rear window. The video finishes with the words, *what does your car say about you?*

I sometimes found the Greenpeace way of doing things a bit too direct and caustic for my non-confrontational sensibilities, so it took me a while to overcome my dislike of some aspects of the advert which I considered to be cheap, unkind and unpleasant – and

---

[1] YouTube. Greenpeace Gas Guzzler video: www.youtube.com/watch?v=h_wMhtuzQKE

still do. I have read suggestions that in consequence of the online flack which was received the film wasn't promoted as widely as had been intended. I fully agree that aspects of its content may have been ill-advised. On the other hand, I don't believe Greenpeace had ever intended endorsing the rather cruel behaviour of the protagonist's office colleagues, which was all part of the shock element. It certainly shocked *me* into taking the issue seriously and the message hit home hard! When I thought about it the Greenpeace way, I realized that I too could justifiably have been called a prick if I'd bought a gas-guzzling vehicle which flattered my ego but was entirely unnecessary. Many other types of large cars were fuel thirsty, of course; but these particular 4x4 vehicles – essentially off-road by design – were increasingly being bought for on-road use, which is why they were being targeted. From then on I became increasingly aware just how many of these ego-flattering vehicles there were on our roads, especially our city roads. It was little wonder that the likes of Freelanders, Range Rovers, Discoveries, Shoguns and Landcruisers acquired the mocking nickname of "Chelsea Tractors".

I think that back in 2007 I would have used the descriptors 4x4 and SUV interchangeably: they were one and the same to me. I thought that all SUVs were four-wheel-drive vehicles. I thought that their off-road capability, even though it might seldom be used, was their main attraction; and even if they weren't going to be used off-road, then their superior all-wheel traction in snowy conditions and on flooded roads was what set them apart. But, truth be told, I hadn't really given the whole subject too much thought. I was aware of there being a certain group of well-to-do people, the Chelsea-Tractor-owning "Sloane Rangers", for example, who bought expensive 4x4s as a kind of superior version of estate car; primarily because of the additional internal space. And I knew from personal experience that being behind the wheel of an elevated vehicle had a feel-good kick to it: I'd once driven a long-wheel-base Defender from Northampton to Canterbury and back; and when asked how I'd got on with it, I truthfully replied that I'd felt like King-of-the-Road! But I wasn't yet aware of how popular 4x4s were becoming as little more, really, than a luxury status symbol. As such, the all-wheel-drive feature was no longer actually essential: for an increasing number of owners, the Sports-Utility feature was what mattered.

I came late to the party of environmentalism as promoted by the likes of Greenpeace and Friends of the Earth. As an individual I'd done my best to be environmentally responsible for most of my adult life. I'd organized litter-picks in the neighbourhood entirely off my own back; I'd forked out a small fortune on long-life light bulbs well before most; I'd supported WWF, the RSPB and the Woodland Trust both financially and as a volunteer; I'd found ways to recycle plastic bottles long before it became vogue to do so; and I was acutely aware of the need to be frugal with the world's precious resources. But it wasn't until I'd begun to become actively involved with Greenpeace that I realized just how far behind I was concerning radical environmental awareness: I hadn't even heard of, let alone read, "The Silent Spring" by Rachel Carson – the book considered by many to be the one that kick-started the modern environmental movement. There was a lot of ground for me to make up, but I think I did so quite quickly. In consequence, I'll not try to deny that my attitude towards fuel-heavy 4x4s soon changed from one of indifference to one of contempt.

Even though now, in 2020, there have been serious improvements to engine efficiency, it doesn't take too much nous to figure out that a Land Rover Discovery, used as an everyday-vehicle, is an environmental menace. Some, with a combined-cycle fuel economy of 44.1 mpg and CO_2 emissions of 170 g/km, compare extremely unfavourably to, say, a popular model of Vauxhall Astra that can achieve 64.2 mpg on a combined cycle with only 90 g/km of CO_2 emissions. As a broad-brush rule of thumb, large 4x4 vehicles have traditionally scored badly against the key indicators of environmental performance, and they continue to do so. Greenpeace's specific issue with 4x4s back in 2007 was attributable to the growing scientific consensus that anthropomorphically generated CO_2 from burning fossil fuels was the most damaging element within the bundle of greenhouse gases responsible for global warming; and the organisation identified climate change as being the greatest global threat to the wellbeing and survival of many animal species. The amount of fossil fuel burnt, Greenpeace argued, needed to be drastically cut back, and a reduction in 4x4 ownership was one way of helping to achieve this objective, even if a small one. Not everyone agreed with this fossil-fuel-reduction analysis of course; but having looked at the evidence for myself, I was more inclined to agree with scientists working for the Intergovernmental Panel on Climate Change than with those increasingly few scientists – along with American presidents and would-be presidents – who begged to differ. And once you begin associating ownership of fuel-heavy vehicles such as the Mitsubishi Shogun with the endangerment of species such as Bengal tigers, it takes on an entirely different, much uglier, aspect.

I was also influenced around the same time by reading about a letter from the British actress, Thandie Newton, in which she invited fellow celebrities to trade in their 4x4s for more environ-mentally friendly vehicles such as the Toyota Prius she herself now owned. As part of a Greenpeace campaign to shame 4x4 owner-ship, volunteer members had been leaving stickers on car wind-screens which read, "this gas-guzzling 4x4 is causing climate change". Newton's own BMW X5 had been stickered and the message reached someone who was receptive to it. She sold the X5 and replaced it with a Toyota Prius, one of the first vehicles to use hybrid technology: it was fitted with a powertrain comprised of a conventional petrol-fuelled internal combustion engine and bat-tery-powered wheel motors. The hybrid powertrain enabled it to achieve improved fuel economy and reduced CO_2 emissions. Newton's epiphany concerning the environmental harm of 4x4s was so complete that she decide to write to other celebrities urging them to ditch their own gas-guzzler. The letter, a collaboration with Greenpeace, included the following comments:

This climate change, which is largely brought on by greenhouse gases in the atmosphere, seriously threatens generations to come...

The hazards I thought I was preventing by driving an SUV are nothing compared to the hazards our children and grandchildren will face if more is not done now...[1]

The circulation list of about 30 celebrities included Chris Martin, Wayne Rooney, Kevin Costner, Tom Cruise, Ozzy Osbourne and Jamie Oliver. I'd never considered buying a 4x4 myself, least of all because I couldn't have afforded to, but I now developed a distinct aversion to them based on my understanding of their being bad news for the environment.

The Leviathan which is a Hummer H3.
Photo from shutterstock.com under licence

Whilst, coincidentally, doing some voluntary campaigning work for Greenpeace myself, I needed to walk past a compound in central London where brand new Hummer H2 and H3 4x4s were being stored. These American vehicles were manufactured by

---

[1] Ohnotheydidn't Live Journal website. "Thandie Newton trades in her climate wrecking BMW": https://ohnotheydidnt.livejournal.com/6274975.html? page=2&mode=reply

General Motors[1] and are best described as massive box-shaped, glossy versions of a military Jeep, completely lacking in any attempt at finesse, brutality being their predominant feature: brutal vehicles for, so I presumed, brutal people. I genuinely felt affronted and alarmed by their sheer size and shape let alone any consideration of what their fuel efficiency, or inefficiency, might be. I've since discovered that an H3 is only capable of a paltry 20 mpg on a combined cycle, and it emits a colossal 327 grams of CO_2 per km.[2]

I recognized, of course, that Hummer 4x4s weren't representative of the whole SUV market, and I was able to quell my disquiet by writing them off as an imported American aberration that wouldn't catch on. I also supposed, in my naivety, that the market for SUVs in general would decline once the stigma of their being associated with global warming became more widespread; after all, there was a similar effect on the demand for large cars back in the seventies when war in the Middle East led to an international fuel crisis and vehicle downsizing became fashionable. The fashion didn't last for too long, however, and was probably more attributable to the huge spike in petrol prices than anything more idealistic. So I'm not quite sure why I thought the SUV fashion trend would be torpedoed by any altruistic concerns for planet earth. From GB car sales of approximately 2.3 million in 2007, only about 183,000 were SUVs; about 8%.[3] At the year's end, there were about 28 million licensed vehicles on British roads, of which just slightly more than 1.5 million were SUVs: about 5%. Their prevalence, therefore, was still limited and I was genuinely

---

[1] They are no longer in production. According to my records, about 120 of them have been registered in the UK. Many of these are, presumably, still being driven on our roads

[2] ultimateSPECS website: www.ultimatespecs.com/car-specs/Hummer/7997/Hummer-H3-37.html

[3] See Appendix 1 for a full explanation of how car sales numbers have been determined. **Car SALES and car REGISTRATIONS are often used interchangeably throughout this discussion even though they may not always be exactly identical – as explained in the appendix.**

hopeful it would reduce rather than grow. I could never have imagined that this kind of vehicle was going to be bought extensively beyond the limited sphere of those who could afford to pay for the status it supposedly conferred.

The Hummer H2 and H3 never really caught on over here. Sadly, there are many equally gross replacements. Take the Ford Ranger double-cab pickup for example. Many, without being able to name the make and model, will have cursed these colossal motors which extend well beyond the allotted length of a supermarket parking space and make re-entry into your own car an act of painful contortion if you come back with your shopping and have the misfortune to find one has parked next to you. Although classified by the Department for Transport as LGVs (Light Goods Vehicles), they are increasingly used as conventional family vehicles; and they are promoted as such by manufacturers who don't miss a trick when it comes to exploiting a potential market. I shall have more to say about these pickups in due course, but, for now, I would simply like to express my opinion that they are the most in-your-face illustration of what is also true about oversized SUVs in general: they are extremely unattractive. Watching the procession of SUVs on our roads today, I often feel like the little boy in the fable of the emperor's new clothes. Why is it that everyone else doesn't seem to recognize what is blindingly obvious, that these SUVs are actually grotesque: grotesque in both size and appearance. Please don't tell me that the sight in your rear-view mirror of an Audi SQ5 bearing down on you doesn't put you in mind of an obese snarling beast. Where is the beauty in a monster?

I recognize, of course, that there is a spectrum, that there are many different shades of SUV grey: some aren't as ugly as others; some even look quite good. But I still think that many people have been hoodwinked by the perversity of fashion – which itself has been manipulated by the marketing strategies of the motor industry – into regarding SUVs as far more attractive than they really are. Although I don't consider myself to be a "car person", I can

Jaguar F-Type coupé: Photo from shutterstock.com under licence

Jaguar F-Pace SUV: Photo from shutterstock.com under licence

recognize the beauty of a classic car when I see one! Jaguar have produced a long line of eye-watering models, the E-type and Mark 2 being up there with the best. I don't believe anyone can seriously think future generations will look back on the Jaguar F-Pace as representative of bygone automotive style and class in the same way the burgundy Mark 2 Jag driven by Inspector Morse is for many today. We're entering the subjective realm, I'm well aware of that; equally aware that my outlook is coloured by my environmental sensitivities. And yet I no more "approve" of a Jensen Interceptor than I do a Maserati Levante. The Interceptor, however, is a vehicle which I find undeniably unique and impressive, whereas the Levante's main stand-out characteristic is its bulk: so far as visual impression is concerned there is little to mark it out from the rest of its upper-class SUV chums. It could be argued that I'm making totally unfair comparisons, like trying to compare a bottle of vintage wine with a magnum of the present year's expensive champagne. Horses for courses; the two cannot be compared. Nonetheless, I stand my ground. Regardless of my ethics, I am perfectly happy to agree that the sleek, graceful lines of today's Jaguar F-Type coupé, for example, are eye-turning; and I feel confident such a verdict will be endorsed by posterity. In contrast, I find the stature of the Jaguar F-Pace SUV with its dominant grill and general bulk to be visually jaw-dropping: it must be near impossible to manufacture something that is primarily *meant* to be bulky and, at the same time, retain those refined characteristics essential to style. I've included two photographs above so my readers can decide for themselves. And as for the Rolls-Royce Cullinan, it has all the grace and poise of a road-roller rather than any other kind of roller. With fuel efficiency of 18.8 mpg, it offends the conscience as well as the sight. I formed this opinion entirely independently of anything I've read, but have since discovered that I'm in good company: apparently BBC Top Gear host, Chris Harris, "can't stand" its looks and has described it as a Chinese knock-off version of itself. In his review of the car, he has echoed the very same thoughts about style that I've just written, wondering as I did so if I was alone. Here's what Harris had to say:

And then there is the way it looks. I had seen pictures and have now seen it in the flesh. I have driven it many miles and have listened to the people who designed it tell me why it looks good. But it doesn't. I think a Rolls-Royce should reek of elegance, and its proportions should leave you breathless with their perfection, just like the Phantom VII did back in 2004. But this car doesn't. I've said before that the subjective world of design and styling is something I prefer not to pass judgement on, but not a single person has told me that they like the way this car looks. [1]

Writing for motor1.com, Clint Simone describes the car like this:

The Rolls-Royce Cullinan is many, many things. Subtle, however, is not one of them. With absolutely massive proportions from just about every angle, the Cullinan is a dominating presence on the road. But... many have asserted that it just isn't very pretty.[2]

Rolls-Royce Cullinan: an unpleasant sight for many.
Shutterstock.com under licence

---

[1] BBC Top Gear website. "Rolls-Royce Cullinan – the Chris Harris verdict": www.topgear.com/car-reviews/rolls-royce/cullinan/5dr-auto/first-drive
[2] Motor1.com website. "Chris Harris can't stand the Rolls-Royce Cullinan's looks": https://uk.motor1.com/news/298716/chris-harris-rolls-royce-cullinan/

Irrespective of its looks, Top Gear's Chris Harris offers his opinion that it's a car which *had* to be built. Why?

There are far too many tasteless rich people for it not to exist.

Thankfully, with prices starting from £276,000, there aren't going to be *too* many of the Cullinans spewing out a criminally high 341 grams of CO_2 every kilometre. I wish there were more people who recognized that what is true of the Cullinan is only, perhaps, the most extreme example of what is true of many other over-sized SUVs: they are intensely unkind to the eye. I've little doubt that many owners and admirers would think I'm missing the whole point in respect to what is and what isn't attractive. After all, by definition a Sport Utility Vehicle has characteristic features in which I have little personal interest: big wheels, big body, elevated driving position and off-road design lineage. It's the attraction of owning and a driving a vehicle that's bigger, roomier, tougher, and more rugged than other vehicles which, for some, maybe for many, lies at the heart of SUV popularity. I'd be hung, drawn and quartered if I tried to suggest that all this is something inherently masculine, an expression of the muscular male ego; so I'll not do so. I might be wrong, but I'm fairly sure that twenty-five years or so ago it was more often than not men who were behind the wheel of large 4x4s. That certainly doesn't seem to be the case any longer. We have a beauty salon of high repute not more than two hundred yards away from our home, and there's nearly always a long line of the beasties – the SUVs, I mean, not the female salon clients – parked outside it on the street. *If* there was a time when the 4x4 market was male dominated, it isn't any longer now that its morphed into an SUV market: the appeal has become thoroughly unisex. Even so, there's little doubt that the attractiveness of an SUV is defined by size, space, stature and strength as much as anything else – either as a collective of characteristics or because one feature – e.g. space – is of particular appeal.[1] Manufacturers recognize this and target their

---

[1] I shall discuss their alleged appeal on safety grounds in Chapter 7.

promotions accordingly. Take these sales pitches from the Renault website for example:

All-New CAPTUR boasts its new muscular design, signature lighting and iconic two-toned body. Bigger with a more expressive design, All-New CAPTUR has an even stronger SUV identity[1]

And,

With its assertive silhouette, muscular shoulders, and imposing front grille, New **KOLEOS** *wins you over at first glance.*[2]

Against all my expectations, and in frustration of all my hopes, the SUV market has boomed since 2007. The 4x4 capability has long since stopped being a defining feature of an SUV, the commonly agreed characteristics being as already mentioned: large wheels, elevated height from ground, wagon-like body style and superior – larger – internal space. Keeping up with the possibilities that the market offers, manufacturers have introduced what are commonly referred to as "crossovers": vehicles which sometimes retain the shape of pre-existing models but have been redesigned to include SUV characteristics, the Mini Countryman being one such example. By introducing SUV crossovers, of course, the market has been extended well beyond the size of what it otherwise would have been. The essential elements of attraction, however, still remain largely the same – as well illustrated by the promotional patter on the Ford website for the "Active" range of vehicles:[3]

If you want a vehicle that looks and feels like a tough SUV but is a bit more compact, then have a look at our new range of Active crossovers. The Focus Active, Fiesta Active and KA+ Active combine the nimble driving dynamics you expect from a smaller car, with the rugged design you'd expect from an SUV.

---

[1] Renault website. "All-new Renault Captur": www.renault.co.uk/cars/all-new-captur.html
[2] Renault website: www.renault.co.uk/cars/koleos.html
[3] Ford website. "Explore Ford Ecosport": www.ford.co.uk/cars/ford-suv

Taking together all those vehicles promoted by manufacturers as a member of the SUV family,[1] there were 975,727 registrations in 2019 – 967,966 were non-electric – from an overall total of 2,295,409 GB car registrations: about 42.5%. The number of licensed cars on British roads had increased to about 32 million by the end of 2019, and roughly 6.1 million of these were SUVs:[2] getting on for 20% – up from about 1.5 million in 2007. In other words, one in every five cars on our 2020 roads is an SUV of some kind, and this proportion continues to increase dramatically year-on-year. *If present trends continue, then nearly half of all new cars bought during 2020 will be SUVs; and by the end of 2028 they will total half of all the cars on our British roads.* These figures are staggering, not least because the growth trend applies as much to larger SUVs as it does to the smaller, crossover SUVs. Take three examples: the Range Rover, the Audi Q5 and the VW Tiguan. These have been chosen purely at random, simply because they have featured on my personal SUV radar as increasingly ubiquitous: and surprisingly so given their price tag. At the beginning of 2010 there were 106,550 Range Rovers on the roads; ten years later, in 2020, this had risen to 391,190. Meanwhile, annual sales have increased from 10,324 to 51,620. Over the same period, the number of Audi Q5s has increased from 5,054 to 81,533, and the number of VW Tiguans from 13,602 to an almost unbelievable 192,594.

I suggest that these trends illustrate a reckless indifference towards the climate emergency looming over the world, and I shall justify my claim with a more detailed quantification in the next few chapters. Engine technology has taken great strides and many SUVs are less gas-guzzling than the 4x4s targeted in the Greenpeace campaign of some thirteen years ago. Taken collectively, however, they remain significantly more environmentally destructive than the alternatives. In my personal view, the boom in sales represents a callous disinterest in the wellbeing of our planet.

---

[1] See appendix 1.
[2] 6,153,494 (6,147,016 non-electric) – calculated from DfT table VEH0128.

CHAPTER THREE
BIG IS THE NEW BEAUTIFUL

I mentioned in the previous chapter that there was a noticeable trend towards vehicle downsizing following the seventies' oil crises. I was a teenager at the time and very muddled in my whole political and social outlook. I do remember, however, being struck by the evidence of my own eyes regarding vehicle preferences and having a respect for those families in my home village who'd "gone small". The small-is-beautiful philosophy promoted by political scientist E. F. Schumacher was making waves – small ones, of course – around the same period: a neat, if coincidental, alignment.

Whilst at university during the last few years of the decade, some friends from the Christian Union introduced me to a musical duo called Fish Co., one half of whom, the artist and actor Steve Farnie, sadly left us when he was far too young. Their first LP, "Can't Be Bad", included a beautiful song – "Children of Tomorrow" – which nostalgically looked back on those who *shed their Brylcreem to become the gentle family*, the ban-the-bomb Aldermaston marches spelling the way for a *newer kind of sensitivity...watched by me*. I myself had also watched the radical social change of the late sixties and early seventies, best understood in my juvenile mind through its expression in popular and progressive music. I was swept along by its tide as an adolescent without *properly* understanding all that was going on around me. Another person who watched it all and *did* understand was the American theologian, Francis Schaeffer. I read some of his work whilst at university and can still remember his description of being left desolate by the collapse of a cultural movement – represented at its extreme by the likes of the Californian Hippies – which, for a while, he'd believed would bring genuine, much-needed change to the prevailing materialistic way of life. Like Jesus, Shaeffer wept. I fully understand and sympathize with his tears. I inwardly weep too, these days, when I think that the same people who frolicked in Woodstock's mud and sang Joni Mitchel's "Big Yellow Taxi" are the very same people who have *paved paradise and put up a parking lot* – lots of them, actually; probably for their SUVs.

I've commented, cynically, that the downsizing of vehicles in the seventies probably had as much to do with the spike in petrol prices as anything else; but I don't think it was the *whole* story. I think there was, genuinely, an aspect of small-is-beautiful to it; an understanding that *all* of the world's resources were scarce, as they still are of course, and changes needed to happen – for self-preservation if not for anything grander. But as surely as the steam which had energized Fish Co's gentle family ran out, so too did the impetus behind downsizing: yet another blow to the hopes Francis Schaefer held for a better world.

Here we are, many decades further on, and my research into what's been happening with GB car sales over the past twenty years would suggest that all vestiges of self-restraint have been well and truly consigned to history. We entered the new millennium with very few genuinely small cars by 1970s' standards; few to compare with the Hillman Imp, the Austin Mini, the Ford Anglia, the first VW Polos, the Renault Reliants, and even the iconic Morris Minor of course. Perhaps we became punch drunk with the availability of larger cars fitted with engines that far exceeded their predecessors in terms of both power *and* fuel efficiency. My own first car was a rusty, rickety, breakdown-prone, greatly-loved, mustard-colour Hillman Imp whose fuel economy was a fraction of the much larger VW Golf which I've owned for the past fourteen years – and which I love equally. Please humour me and allow me to make a very brief observational comment about Morris Minors; an observation which is entirely gratuitous and possibly controversial. It's one of just two or three anecdotal digressions throughout this discussion, and I'm including it for nothing more than a love of these wonderfully unpretentious masterworks of British design and manufacturing. Jeanne's first car was a beautiful olive-green 1966 model, and would-to-god that she'd never sold it just a few years before we met in 1981. I once belonged to a residential community with a shared carpool that included a Morris Minor. One man commented that when he was behind its wheel he could find no "pride of life" whatsoever. Didn't that man have any soul, I wonder? With its wonderful spoked steering wheel, its upright seats and its distinctive engine throb, I personally felt it was a delight to drive. Those were the days, of course, when you could tell what car was coming down the road by the sound of its engine; you really could. I miss all of that! I was quite surprised to discover that there are still over 14,000 of them on the roads today. Maybe one of them will come up for sale at the right price?

Jeanne (c1978) with her 1966 Morris Minor – note the flares! © John Everett

The move away from small cars has been quite phenomenal; far more than I would ever have realized from observation alone. Ford Ka sales were nearly 67,000 in 2002. Since then they have more or less gone down year-on-year, except between 2012 and 2015 when numbers fluctuated – and also when there was a brief resurgence in 2017. In 2019 there were just less than 6,000 registrations.[1] Imagine how steep the decline would look on the sales graph at a Ford Motors' board meeting! Let me reiterate, just for emphasis. *Sales of the Ford Ka in 2019 have declined to just 9% of what they were in 2002; from nearly 67,000 a year to less than 6,000.* And it's not just that the Ka itself has probably become unpopular as a model, the same trend applies to most of its small(ish) peers. The Nissan Micra hit peak sales of 51,633 in 2003. Since then it has shown a similar downward trend, and in 2019 sales were a meagre 8,564. The Fiat Panda – what a car! – showed resurgent sales between 2004 and 2009, with annual totals rising from 8,841 to 13,330. In 2019, however, sales were down to 2,579. Like its giant mammal namesake, the car would appear to be a critically endangered species; and numbers have surely fallen below the point where survival is possible. The popular Honda Jazz and Vauxhall Corsa have both slid down the same slippery sales-slope: the Jazz from 30,138 in 2006 to 16,740 in 2019; and the Corsa from a 2008 high of 98,076 to a low of 51,717 in 2017. The fall has since stabilized somewhat, and 53,942 Corsas were sold in 2019. Even the fashionably chic "Cinquecento" Fiat 500, probably the smallest of the bunch, has seen sales fall from a 2014 peak of 52,978 to 21,516 in 2019.

By way of taking a breather from the relentless spew of numbers, perhaps it would be a good time to make the observation that an SUV crossover based on the Fiat 500 – the 500X – had its first full year of sales in 2015, when 7,400 cars were registered. Interestingly, this is more or less equivalent to the reduction in

---

[1] This figure is made up largely of Ford Ka+ sales. It excludes the Ka Active, which I have designated as an SUV crossover. Introduction of the "Active" crossover range most probably results from an effort to curb falling sales.

registrations of its smaller sibling. I have to confess that I don't "get it"; isn't the diminutive size an essential feature of the Fiat 500? It's not as if you're getting the best of both worlds from the crossover model is it: the benefits of an SUV together with the retro experience of driving a Fiat Cinquecento copy? All that's left if you buy a 500X is a vague, very vague, resemblance in terms of shape. So too if you buy an, ahem, "Mini" Clubman. Excuse me! It isn't a Mini any longer in any sense of the word.

The VW Up!, another genuinely small car, has also been a casualty of the decline in fortune for the nippers. Introduced in 2012, it saw peak sales in 2014 of 20,931. In 2019 the figures were 8,238. And last but not least, the Ford Fiesta: the market leader by a country mile and another of those cars which used to be genuinely small back in the day. It no longer, however, enjoys heady six-figure sales: the 2015 peak of 131,367 annual registrations was never to be even nearly challenged in the following years, least of all by the 67,634 sales figure for 2019;[1] nearly half what it had been just five years previously. Only a few models have bucked the trend, one of them being the VW Polo. Sales have remained fairly stable at between 40,000 and 50,000 each year, as they have for its budget-range equivalent – the Skoda Fabia. For the sake of completeness and to ensure that my analysis is as robust as possible, I should also mention the Kia Picanto – a vehicle whose diminutive size is matched by its price: the manufacturer's website lists the price as starting from £10,192.[2] An initial registration-peak of 15,454 was reached in 2009, followed by a post-financial-crisis nadir of 11,966 in 2011. Annual registrations have since fluctuated between about 12,000 and 15,000, and they reached a new high of 17,559 in 2019. This all suggests that there are some remaining car buyers who will opt for a smaller vehicle either as their longstanding car of choice or if, as they say, the price is right.

---

[1] See footnote 1 from page 32 concerning the "Active" range of cars.
[2] Kia Motors website (July 2020). New Cars page. Range: www.kia.com/uk/new-cars

I ought also, very briefly, to draw attention to the concurrent decline in sales of popular medium-size car models, which must have been another cause of alarm for the manufacturers. The Vauxhall Astra is a good example. Registrations have literally nosedived from the giddy height of 111,586 in 2007 to 22,448 in 2019. Its larger sibling, the popular Insignia, saw registrations fall from 31,664 in 2012 to 8,205 in 2018. I'm no fan of the Insignia, which I've not enjoyed driving on the two or three occasions when I've been allocated one as an Enterprise hire-car, but I could almost become broody about its poor fortune when it's set in the context of SUV increases: Vauxhall SUV and SUV-crossover sales rose from 8,053 in 2012 to 60,730 in 2019.

Few types of small and medium-size cars, it seems, are safe from the growing world-wide dominance of SUVs. That the craze for these vehicles began in the USA is a quite-probably-true popular concept. To blame, we have the Jeep Cherokee; a successor to the Jeep Wagoneer which retained its off-road capabilities. By the time the Cherokee was launched in 1984 the British Range Rover was a well-established 4x4, but – as with the popular Toyota Land Cruiser – it had a comparatively small, restricted, niche market during the eighties and nineties and wasn't in any way considered a mass-production rival to saloons, sedans, hatchbacks and estates. The Cherokee, however, was! Branded by Jeep as a "sportswagon", it sold three million units before production stopped in 2001. Hot on its heels, in 1991, came the Ford Explorer, manufactured in a range of different configurations intended as a lure to the "sporty" sector of the market as well as the "utility" sector. In 1993 it became a USA top-ten bestseller, and the modern SUV was born.[1] The Toyota Rav4 was probably the most popular trailblazer for a crossover of SUV popularity into European and Asian car-buying culture, and the first decade of this century saw a rush for car manufacturers to exploit potential profits from the motor sectors' very own gold rush: the

---

[1] Concept Car Credit website. "The History of the SUV": www.conceptcarcredit.co.uk/the-history-of-the-suv

Nissan Qashqai, which has gone on to become Nissan's most popular European car, demonstrated the scale of lucrative demand for what we now know as compact SUVs. The tsunami of SUV sales isn't restricted to Europe; it's had a global impact. An Australian on-line car magazine article will distress those of us who regard this world takeover as being unhealthy, especially in the way it kills off any smaller rivals standing in its path. In August 2017, carsales.com ran the following headline and article:

Meet T-Roc, VW's new baby SUV: Styling shakeup as Volkswagen joins the junior crossover battle.

The Golf has been the cornerstone of Volkswagen's worldwide sales juggernaut since the 1970s, but it's finally showing signs of slowing. Enter the T-Roc.

A compact crossover built to take the Golf's interior size package and make it taller, the T-Roc is the third member of Volkswagen's SUV family, positioned below the bigger new Tiguan, which will spawn the 2018 Tiguan Allspace, and the Touareg, which will be renewed next year.[1]

For a few years following the financial crisis of 2008,[2] total GB car registrations fell to under 2 million. But apart from during these years, registrations from 2001 to 2018 have consistently been between about 2.2 million and 2.5 million: there has been no evidence of any significant increase or decrease. Given the growth in SUV ownership that has already been referenced,[3] the inescapable conclusion is that many people are opting to buy an SUV *in preference* to the smaller high-demand cars they would previously have done. If this were not the case, then *total* car sales

---

[1] Carsales website. News page. "Cheaper Volkswagen T-Roc confirmed": www.carsales.com.au/editorial/details/meet-t-roc-vws-new-baby-suv-108562

[2] 2009 to 2012.

[3] In Chapter 2, I commented that SUV registrations had grown from about 183,000 in 2007 to just over 975,000 in 2019.

figure would inevitably have been noticeably higher year-on-year to reflect the surge in SUV sales.

It wouldn't be unreasonable to argue, of course, that this trend for larger, more expensive cars is possibly reflective of a general increase in wealth spread across the population as a whole. Data released by the Office for National Statistics (ONS) allows us to plot changes to the median household disposable income. Put at its simplest, this measure of income reflects what the "average household" has at its disposal to spend after statutory payments such as income tax have been deducted. "Average income" in this context is the median – the income for a family who find themselves in the central position where 50% of the nation's families earn more than they do, and 50% earn less. The income figures provided by the ONS are "equivalised", which means they have been adjusted for different numbers of people within a household so that they remain representative. In the financial year 2018/2019 the figure was £29,600, up from £23,200 in 2000/2001; an increase of £6,400 – nearly 28%.[1]

It would be helpful to try and compare this trend with increases in specific car prices; but comparing like-for-like is almost impossible. The bestselling line of Range Rovers in 2018, for example, was the Evoque HSE TD4 auto. This line wasn't in production back in 2001 when the bestseller was the Vogue Auto. To try and compare these two models would be almost like trying to compare two entirely different vehicles. The best I've been able to do by way of making a meaningful assessment of any relationship between rising disposable income and expenditure on vehicles is to utilize information from "statista", a statistics website which, amongst much else, provides Consumer Price Index information for new

---

[1] Office for National Statistics: (i) Average Household Income, UK: Financial year ending 2019. (ii) Mean and median equivalized disposable income by age of individual, 2000/01 to 2017/18, UK.

car purchases in the UK from 2007 to 2019.[1] Taking 2015 as the base year (100), we can trace an increase from 88.4 in 2007 to 112.2 in 2019. Expressed differently, new car prices have risen about 27% since 2007, a little over 2% per year. Extending this trend backwards, we may reasonably suppose that the increase in prices from 2002 to 2019 will have been about 38 to 40%, which is considerably higher than the 28% rise in household disposable income that took place between 2001/2002 and 2018/2019: *in other words, there isn't any reason to suppose the huge increase in purchase of SUVs has been because households have found that buying a new car has become less financially demanding and have consequently been able to consider buying bigger, more expensive vehicles than they were previously able to.* I've not specifically explored the possibility that SUVs have, as a category of vehicle, followed a lower inflationary trend to that of new vehicles in general and therefore become *comparatively* more affordable, but nor have I come across any evidence in the course of my research to suggest that such an explanation might be plausible.

Dusting down and donning my economics degree mortar board, I can identify the demand-curve for SUVs as becoming increasingly inelastic: in other words, demand is less responsive to price than one would expect. The conventional demand curve – or line – for goods and services, with price shown on the vertical axis and demand on the horizontal axis, slopes diagonally downwards from left to right. It's the economic science's way of expressing in a graph what we all know intuitively: the cheaper a product, the more of it gets sold; and as its price rises, so the demand for it falls. In the most basic conventional scenario, the *assumed* relationship – the standard bearer of economic analysis – between the price of a product and demand for it is uniform: if the price doubles, then the demand halves. A more *elastic* demand curve,

---

1 Statista website. Statistics page. "Consumer price index of new car purchases annually in the United Kingdom (UK) from 2007 to 2019": www.statista.com/ statistics/286563/consumer-price-index-cpi-of-new-car-purchases-annual-average-uk

however, is less steep. It tells us that small differences in price will have a greater impact on demand: put up the price of a product by just a small amount and the effect on sales will be considerable. Received economic wisdom typically characterizes the market for cars as being noticeably elastic: given the choices available, an increase in the price of any particular vehicle will have a significant impact on its sales as customers switch to alternative models. Specific customer loyalties, of course, established over many years (as in the case of those towards, for example, the Ford Fiesta), can create distortions. In general, however, the elastic correlation holds good. But the demand curve for models within the SUV grouping would appear to have veered towards inelasticity: it has steepened. In other words, customers are less concerned about price when purchasing any given SUV model than might normally be supposed. Higher prices don't appear to have deterred sales as much as would normally be expected. I think you only have to look around and see the number of Range Rover Evoques, Land Rover Discoveries, Kia Sportages, Audi Q5s, BMW X5s, Nissan Qashqais, and VW Tiguans parked in your street compared to ten years ago to see the visible corroboration of this economic assessment.

SUV Central...just along from road from where I live. Price doesn't seem to have impacted SUV sales as might have been expected: an example of price inelasticity. © John Everett

Even whilst having to dig more deeply into their pockets, car buyers are essentially giving two fingers to environmental concerns as they fork out for the must-have SUVs which will satisfy their demand. Take sales of the Lexus NX SUV and the Lexus IS saloon as examples. I've chosen these because their entry price on the Lexus website is *reasonably* close and they would both appear to serve a similar market. The IS model is described as a "hybrid dynamic sports saloon" and is available from £33,265.[1] Fuel economy in the model range is given as between 44.8 and 48.7 mpg on a combined cycle; and CO_2 emissions are given as between 133 and 144 g/km. Alternatively, the NX SUV would cost from £35,860 and has inferior fuel economy at between 36.6 and 39.7 mpg. It also has higher CO_2 emissions of between 161 and 175 g/km. On the basis of both financial and environmental considerations the IS saloon would appear to be the winner. And yet although registrations were roughly equal in 2015 at 3,550 for the IS and 3,626 for the NX, by 2019 NX registrations far outstripped the IS: 4,662 compared to 1,232.

Sales of the Kia Sportage, a well-established and popular SUV, also point in the same direction. The closest alternative range, by price, within the Kia marque is the Ceed, which includes an estate car version: the Ceed Sportswagon – neatly but misleadingly named to presumably identify it as belonging to the Jeep Cherokee lineage. The Ceed car is promoted by Kia as being a cut above other ones, suitable for those who want a vehicle that announces itself:

The Kia Ceed instantly grabs your attention: the bold design features a front grille framed by full LED headlights and striking 'Ice Cube' LED Running Lights, a chrome window line and 17" alloy wheels. In short, the Kia Ceed has everything you need to put the fun back into driving.[2]

---

[1] Lexus website (July 2020). Cars: www.lexus.co.uk/car-models
[2] Kia Motors (July 2020). New Cars page. Range: www.kia.com/uk/new-cars

And this is how the estate car version is described:

Need more room to enjoy your day? Meet the Kia Ceed Sportswagon. It combines assured, athletic design with an abundance of space and a dynamic drive. At the front, it shares the hatchback's design credentials, while the low, sleek profile with its chrome window surrounds extend further than ever before. Plus, the additional boot space with folding rear seats allow you the freedom to add whatever you need. So let nothing stop you.

In short, the Ceed range is marketed as being of appeal to the discerning; a genuine alternative for potential SUV customers who might still be considering their options. The fuel economy for the entry-level hatchback is reported to be from 38.2 mpg and its emissions from 99 g/km. For the estate car version, the corresponding figures are 44.1 mpg and 109 g/km; prices are from £18,885 and £19,885 respectively. In contrast, corresponding information about the Kia Sportage would appear – on paper at least – to be unfavourable: fuel economy from 31.7 mpg, CO_2 emissions from 117 g/km, and a price tag from £21,010. Imagine that you have £21k or so to spend on a new vehicle and have a choice to make between the Ceed range of cars – which includes a spacious estate car model – or the Sportage range of SUVs. The warranty and service provision will, of course, be exactly the same for whichever vehicle is chosen. Would it not be the case that anyone who has a concern for both economy and the environment would opt for the Ceed? You'd surely think so, wouldn't you? In 2012, Ceed registrations across the complete range were 13,305. Sportage registrations were 14,161 and registrations of all Kia Motors' cars totalled nearly 70,000. By 2014 Sportage numbers had increased to 20,690, Ceed numbers had fallen to 11,230, and the Kia Motors' total was 72,470. By 2016 the SUV craze had really gone into overdrive, if I can use an automotive descriptor for it. Kia Motors' executives were congratulating themselves with a leap in total registrations to nearly 84,000, driven by Sportage sales which had leapt to just shy of 39,000! Three years later in

2019, from a company sales total of 94,464, Ceed sales were a lowly 10,217 and Sportage numbers had also dropped back slightly to 33,657. A drop in the SUV sales figures might have been welcome environmental news except that the fall was most likely explained by a new budget-SUV having been introduced into the Kia Motors' range: the Stonic. It sold 8,160 in 2019 – its second full registration year – which more than offset the slight dip in Sportage sales. As a pertinent aside: of the 94,464 Kia Motors' cars sold in 2019, 45,501 were SUVs – very nearly 50 percent.

On the basis that car buyers have been increasingly expressing a preference for vehicles which have a poorer fuel economy and higher CO_2 emissions than possible alternatives, I think I can claim to have established that the surge in UK SUV ownership has been an environmentally unfriendly one. I'm hardly a lone voice crying out in the wilderness: the problem has long been recognized by European policy makers, as reflected in a report from "Transport & Environment" (T&E) – a Brussels-based not-for-profit institute which, supported by 62 global organisations, researches, debates and campaigns on issues concerning…that's right: transport and environment. Responding to a study from the European Environment Agency, which reported a small rise in CO_2 emissions from new cars in 2017, T&E published an article in May 2018 with the headline:

Rise in car CO_2 emissions last year due to surging SUV sales, not declining diesel [1]

Car manufacturers had been complaining that it would be difficult for them to meet stringent new European regulations on vehicle emissions because of declining diesel sales in the wake of Dieselgate, the emissions-cheating scandal triggered by VW. Taken

---

[1] Transport & Environment website. News: www.transportenvironment.org/news/rise-car-co2-emissions-last-year-due-surging-suv-sales-not-declining-diesel-%E2%80%93-analysis

in general, diesel engines have a more favourable bill of CO_2 health; so declining sales will possibly have an adverse impact on the average CO_2 emissions figures for fleet sales. The article carried on:

Last week's confirmation that the average CO_2 emissions of a new car sold in the EU increased in 2017 is the result of carmakers selling more SUVs, crossovers and more powerful vehicles.

It's not the most clearly written sentence, but it confirms the point that increased emissions are directly attributable to *more* SUV sales, not *less* diesel sales. In a nutshell, the sales bonanza of SUVs has been environmentally unhealthy. A report on the consequences of the new European laws, written by Hilton Holloway for Autocar magazine, also recognizes SUVs as the villains of the piece:

The market shift towards SUVs could make it near impossible for car makers to meet the laws.[1]

Egged on by the manufacturers, car buyers have been making choices which represent a flagrant disregard for our collective need to reduce CO_2 emissions and cut back on our fuel consumption. Perhaps the SUV growth-trend would at least be more understandable if it were driven by the need to make hard financial choices, if buying SUVs was predicated on the need for British families to cut costs. There is, however, no evidence that points us in this direction; quite the opposite. *British car buyers, it seems, are increasingly willing to actually pay **a premium** for a machine which helps to trash the world.*

---

[1] Autocar magazine website. Car news page. "Analysis – How will car makers meet new CO_2 laws?": www.autocar.co.uk/car-news/industry/analysis-how-will-car-makers-meet-new-co2-laws

Chapter Four
SUV Inefficiency.

The introduction of crossover SUVs, often just called crossovers, has undoubtedly broadened the appeal of the category in general, and I assume it must be increasingly difficult for the crossover-buying public to feel that their own vehicle is "worse" than any other one. The differences do, indeed, become marginal. Take the Ford Fiesta *Active* as an example. The online Autocar magazine review sets out the differences to its baby sister – the Fiesta – like this:

"... it rides 18mm higher and has a bit of cladding around the outside to make it look more rufty-tufty. Like a jelly baby wearing walking boots. Suspension is modified to suit and the tracks are 10mm wider and tyre profiles tend to be a little higher."[1]

Cutting to the quick, it's bigger, higher, and it's got a more – to use that wonderful Autocar adjective – rufty-tufty feel. The trade-off for getting your money's worth of extra rufty-tufty-ness, however, is that you end up owning a car which is marginally worse for the environment. The specifications given by Autocar magazine for comparative models of Fiesta and Fiesta Active, both fitted with a 1.0 Ecoboost 125 engine, indicate a decrease in combined-cycle fuel efficiency from 57.7 mpg to 56 mpg, and a corresponding increase in CO_2 emissions from 108 g/km to 114 g/km respectively. This is definitely getting into split-hairs territory, but all I'm doing at present is introducing an issue that we shall soon discover has genuine import. The case is made to be somewhat more convincing

---

[1]   Autocar: Car Reviews. "Ford Fiesta Active": www.autocar.co.uk/car-review/ford/fiesta-active

if we look at the Ford Ecosport, which is several notches further up the SUV scale than the Fiesta Active and more distinctly identifiable as one by both size and shape. Performance information for a 5-door model fitted with the same 1.0 Ecoboost engine is exactly as one would predict: a further decrease in fuel efficiency to 53 mpg and significantly higher CO_2 emissions of 140 g/km – CO_2 emissions are inversely related to fuel economy; as mpg readings decrease, CO_2 readings increase.

I would be setting myself up as a straw man to be knocked down if I didn't acknowledge that there are subtle shadings to all of this. Some dear friends came to visit us not so long ago and arrived in their Mercedes GLA, the infant of the Mercedes SUV family. At 4.4 metres in length, and a width of 2.02 metres (including mirrors), it fitted neatly onto our drive; not so very different to our VW Golf, which is 4.26 metres long and 2.03 metres wide. The GLA's 17" wheels and body shape give it a more elevated look than that of the Golf, which makes do with humble 15" wheels. But the differences aren't enough for Jeanne to have identified it as an SUV; she showed the same surprise that many would, I guess, when I told her that it was included on the SUV section of the Mercedes website.

I'll happily concede that the GLA isn't anywhere near as aggressive looking as, say, the latest model of Land Rover Discovery, and my friends might well have said it was a case of the pot calling the kettle black if I'd ventured to criticize them for owning one. But even though my reasons for disliking SUVs become less defensible when applied to the smaller crossover models, I still remain concerned about the widespread aspiration to own a vehicle – *any* vehicle – which is a member of the SUV family. Manufacturers have responded to the aspirational demand signals being sent out from buyers by supplying them with a wide range of models which they are able to market under the generic SUV category heading, the result being that there has been a literal stampede to own vehicles which collectively herald bad news.

Whist in hunt for clarification about crossovers, I came across the definition of an SUV as given by that august body, the RAC. Belatedly, I reproduce it here given that it rather neatly confirms and justifies the rationale I've been using for SUV classification:

SUV, or sports utility vehicle, has become an umbrella term for a variety of hardy vehicles including crossovers, 4x4s and off-roaders.

Initially, SUVs were big, four-wheel drive machines built for rugged terrains, with a powerful engine, large boot and spacious interior. While some are still made for life off-road, many modern SUVs are designed only to be used on the tarmac.

What they do all offer, however, is a comfortable, solid drive at motorway speeds. Many are just as easy to drive as a family hatchback, and smaller models and hybrids are perfect for zipping around town. They have sturdy bodies and sit a bit higher off the ground which, as well as making you feel more in control, can make it easier for people with mobility issues to get in and out.

Examples: Mazda CX5, Nissan Qashqai, Kia Sorento, Land Rover Discovery

Ever helpful, the RAC then tells us that this group of vehicles would be *perfect for…*

"families with large dogs who enjoy walks on remote beaches and adventures in the great outdoors."[1]

Hmmm! Are the SUVs perfect for *large dogs* who enjoy walks on remote beaches or for the *families* who do so? It doesn't seem to be clear, which just shows the care writers need to take in order

---

[1]   RAC website. Drive page. "Coupe or hatchback? A guide to different car types": https://www.rac.co.uk/drive/advice/buying-and-selling-guides/guide-to-different-car-types

to avoid using misplaced modifiers, a grammatical trap constantly waiting to ensnare the unwary. I'm greatly indebted to the Collins "Good Grammar" paperback, which has re-taught me most of what never really sunk in when I was at school. If we assume that the modifier relates to families and you fit the adventuring-criteria bill, then the RAC seems to be suggesting that an SUV would be the perfect vehicle to accommodate your lifestyle choices. It doesn't, however, make any comment about the environmental impact of using your SUV for, say, the daily two-mile school run on urban roads.

Apart from lamenting the insidious increase in general vehicle size which has taken place over several decades, and disliking the sheer bulk of many SUVs specifically, what case can I offer for being such a party-pooper about a class of vehicle which is clearly popular with so many? The high-emissions factor is key to it all, an issue I've already referred to in several places but which I'd now like to explore in some detail. The most obvious aspect to consider is what is known as "tailgate emissions": essentially, that's all the gases coming out of a vehicle's exhaust pipe. We don't see the CO_2, of course, because it's colourless; as is its cousin, carbon monoxide (CO), the invisible killer which is often connected to faulty boilers as well as exhaust fumes. Dispersed in the atmosphere, it doesn't form any specific health risk or act as a greenhouse gas (GHG). It does, however, contribute to the formation of tropospheric ozone, an unhealthy pollutant. Recent satellite tracing of pollutants indicates an association between atmospheric CO concentrations and other GHGs, but I'm unable to offer any more detailed observations on the subject.[1]

Most of us these days will know that cars emit other pollutants which have a direct bearing on air quality and, most notoriously, can lead to urban smog. The six pollutants which, collectively,

---

[1] For those interested, further reading can be found on the Nasa website. "Fourteen years of carbon monoxide from MOPITT." Adam Voiland: https://climate.nasa.gov/news/2291/fourteen-years-of-carbon-monoxide-from-mopitt

form the basis of air-quality measurement are: carbon monoxide, lead, nitrogen oxides, ground-level ozone, particle pollution (often referred to as particulate matter), and sulphur oxides. With the exception of lead – since the year 2000 – and ozone, all of these are present as a by-product of combusting petrol and diesel in car engines. Benzene is another vehicle pollutant of concern, especially on account of its carcinogenic properties. I can do little better at this juncture than to copy-and-paste what the RAC website tells us about vehicle emissions:

- *Carbon dioxide (CO_2)* – *CO_2 is a greenhouse gas, thought to be a major contributing factor to climate change. Although technically non-toxic, excessive volumes contribute towards ocean acidification.*
- *Carbon monoxide (CO)* – *This invisible gas is the result of incomplete combustion of fuel and is very toxic to humans. Most modern engines only produce tiny amounts of it thanks to efficient combustion processes, but older engines are bigger offenders.*
- *Nitrogen oxides (NOx)* – *Nitrogen oxides are produced in any combustion process. They are highly reactive and can contribute to smog when they come into contact with other airborne chemicals. Some manufacturers famously cheated NOx tests.*
- *Sulfur dioxide (SO2)* – *This is a colourless gas that smells like burnt matches and occurs naturally in crude oil used to refine petrol and diesel. It forms acids when burned, leading to engine corrosion and smog.*
- *Hydrocarbons (HC)* – *HCs escape from exhausts as unburnt fuel due to incomplete combustion. They also evaporate from the fuel tank and nozzle when you fill up at the petrol station.*
- *Benzene (C6H6)* – *This occurs naturally in petrol and diesel in very small quantities and is also emitted from vehicle exhausts as unburnt fuel. Benzene is a carcinogenic substance and high levels of inhalation can severely harm human health.*
- *Particulates* – *Diesel engines emit airborne particles of black soot and metal, known as particulate matter. Modern cars are*

fitted with diesel particulate filters (DPFs) to stop these harmful particles being pumped out into the atmosphere.[1]

It isn't my intention to explore the impact of each of these vehicle emissions – CO_2 excluded – in great depth, save to make the obvious point that if SUVs in general have an inferior fuel efficiency to non-SUVs, then it isn't just the owners who are taking a hit – a financial one – at every visit to the filling station; we're *all* taking a hit by virtue of the increased contribution to poor air quality from the combustion of the extra fuel; especially so when these leviathans are being used around town. Our health is hugely important, of course, but my objection to SUVs has never really been predicated on their being any more polluting than other vehicles. To a large degree the problem with excessive NOx emissions, for example, is their impact on humans, especially for those who live and work in urban areas. Other animals will be affected too, but not always to the same degree as humankind is. As such, the pollutants aspect of our love affair with cars in general, and SUVs in particular, isn't one which is directly contributory to the apocalyptic weather patterns that will overwhelm the earth and all its life forms if global warming becomes too severe, even if it has extremely serious implications for the health and wellbeing of both flora and fauna. Without belittling the pollution issue, it isn't the one which I can own to having got under my skin. It's a problem which I don't claim to have researched thoroughly and it would be disingenuous if I tried commandeering it to buttress other issues which trouble me. I haven't made specific enquiry about levels of NOx emissions from different vehicles, and I wouldn't wish to go beyond re-emphasising the correlation between vehicle fuel economy and tailgate emissions in general.

Central to my analysis of SUV tailgate CO_2 emissions will be comparisons with other types of car, which, for simplicity, I've

---

[1] RAC website. Drive page. "Is my car bad for the environment? A guide to vehicle exhaust emissions": https://www.rac.co.uk/drive/advice/emissions/vehicle-exhaust-emissions-what-comes-out-of-your-cars-exhaust

grouped together as one. Finding a suitable name for this coalition type, however, has proved tricky. Initially, I started calling them non-SUVs; but it led to clumsy word repetition. I then thought about using "Ordinary Vehicles"; but I'm well aware that some of the cars are far from ordinary and would have felt hard done by. "General Vehicle" seemed to be more apt and I decided to use it. The abbreviation to GV, however, could easily be read as Goods Vehicle, as in the Light Goods Vehicle (LGV) licencing category. To settle the matter, then, I'm proud to introduce GEN-V into the automotive lexicon as the abbreviated label for the grouping of general vehicles: the coalition of all non-SUVs within the car category.

I would also, for the avoidance of doubt in my terminology, like to use the animal kingdom taxonomy as a point of comparison for the hierarchy of names within the vehicle nomenclature. Mammals are one class of vertebrate animal. Within this class there are various species; dogs are one of them: a pertinent illustration, possibly, given our main topic of discussion – I've often heard ageing cars referred to as "old dogs". Drilling down, we find different breeds of dog such as terriers or collies. And, finally, there are different lines within the breeds; a rough collie, for example, being the most commonly-owned type – or line – of collie. In a similar kind of hierarchy, the car is one particular class of motor vehicle. Within this class there are quite a few different types (species), including the SUV, the saloon, the sedan, the estate and the hatchback. I haven't included all the different types and I wonder, purely as an idle thought, how many of us could explain the difference between a sedan and a saloon? A good quiz question, maybe, but not important in this context. Different manufacturers often have many types of vehicle in their range; some, such as Land Rover, specialize in only one particular type. Types of vehicle are further subdivided into models (breeds): the Ford Fiesta and the VW Polo are both models within the hatchback vehicle type. Finally, models will have different lines, typically characterized by different engines and a different array of features (often known as trims).

Make & model (in bold), and line	CO$_2$ (g/ km)	mpg **	Kerb Weight (kg)	Length (m)	Width (m)	List Price (£)	Euro NCAP Safety (%)				2018 "line" numbers	2018 "model" numbers
							A	B	C	D		
Nissan Qashqai: 1.2 DiG-T N-Connecta [Comfort Pack] 5dr	129	50.4	1,498	4.37	2.07	23325	88	83	69	79	11,795	49,288
Land Rover Range Rover Evoque: 2.0 TD4 HSE Dynamic 5dr Auto	168	44.1	1,746	4.37	2.09	44295	94	87	72	73	4,541	49,106
Ford Kuga: 2.0 TDCi Titanium Edition 5dr 2WD	152	48.7	1,716	4.53	2.09	28,080	92	86	82	73	7,633	38,956
Kia Sportage: 1.6 GDi ISG 2 5dr	156	41.6	1,490	4.48	2.08	22,185	90	83	66	71	6,782	34,562
Vauxhall Mokka: X 1.6CDTi ecoTEC D 136 Active 5dr	127	50.4	1,409	4.28	2.04	22,360	96	90	67	100	9,148	31,530
Volkswagen Tiguan: 1.4 TSi BMT 150 SE Nav 5dr	131	48.7	1,750	4.48	2.1	26,785	96	84	72	68	3,678	30,884
Land Rover Discovery: Sport 2.0 TD4 180 HSE 5dr Auto	170	44.1	1,954	4.59	2.17	40,715	93	83	69	82	3,470	27,958
Hyundai Tucson: 1.6 GDi Blue Drive SE Nav 5dr 2WD	147	44.8	1,379	4.47	2.06	22,550	86	85	71	71	5,796	26,316
Nissan Juke: 1.0 DiG-T Tekna 5dr	118	55.4	1,199	4.21	1.98	22,270	94	85	81	73	4,490	24,027
Ford Ecosport: 1.0 EcoBoost 125 ST-Line 5dr	114	53.3	1,205	4.1	2.06	20,725	93	77	58	55	6,453	22,238
Weighted Average (All)	143	48	1,562	Safety Average			92	84	71	75	Total	334,865
Weighted Average (Top 3)	149	48	1,648			Worst	A = Adult Occupant					
Weighted Average (Top 6)	145	47	1,606			Best	B = Child Occupant					
** mpg data relates to EC "combined cycle"						Highest	C = Vulnerable Road User					
						Lowest	D = Safety Assist					

Table 1: Top-ten bestselling SUVs in 2018 as compiled from Department for Transport Vehicle Licensing statistics, Table VEH0160 (updated 19/12/2019). Additional vehicle-specific data courtesy BBC Top Gear online vehicle reviews.

Table 1, above, contains information for the top-ten bestselling SUVs in 2018, listed by the most popular line within the model range. Table 2, below, provides an identical data-set of information for the top-ten GEN-Vs. Comparison of the two data sets shows that the SUVs produce considerably more CO_2 emissions than the GEN-Vs, and they also have considerably inferior fuel economy figures.[1] For SUVs, the CO_2 range (in g/km) is from a best of 114 (Ford Ecosport) to a worst of 170 (Land Rover Discovery). The weighted average for all ten is 143 g/km. These figures contrast with a GEN-V CO_2 best (in g/km) of 90 (Vauxhall Astra) to a worst of 127 (Ford Fiesta), with a weighted average for all ten of 111: 32 g/km (22%) less, or better, than the SUV figure. Similarly, the best SUV for fuel consumption (EC combined cycle: mpg) at 55.4 is the Nissan Juke, and the worst at 41.6 is the Kia Sportage. The weighted average for all is 48 mpg. For GEN-Vs, the best car for fuel consumption at 72.3 mpg is the Toyota Yaris,[2] and the Ford Fiesta worst at 51.4. The weighted average for all GEN-Vs is 59: 11 mpg (23%) more, or better, than the SUV figure.

---

[1] A full explanation of calculations is given in Appendix 2

[2] A popular-selling line of Toyota Yaris is fitted with a hybrid engine (a smaller version of the one in the previously mentioned Toyota Prius), which accounts for it being "best of group". Not ALL Yaris models have this engine, so I weighted the data accordingly. A full explanation of how I did so is given in Appendix 2. None of the most popular lines (or trims) of the SUVs had hybrid engines.

Make & model (in bold), and line	CO_2 (g/ km)	mpg **	Kerb Weight (Kg)	Length (m)	Width (m)	List Price (£)	Euro NCAP Safety (%)				2018 "line" numbers	2018 "model" numbers
							A	B	C	D		
Ford Fiesta: 1.0 EcoBoost Zetec 5dr	110	58.9	1,163	4.04	1.94	16,515	87	84	64	60	18,576	90,225[1]
Volkswagen Golf: 1.5 TSI EVO SE [Nav] 5dr	113	56.5	1,280	4.26	2.03	21,930	95	89	76	78	5,422	61,362[2]
Vauxhall Corsa: 1.2 Energy 3dr [AC]	124	53.3	1,166	4.02	1.94	12,545	79	77	71	56	8,967	52,455
Ford Focus: 1.5 EcoBoost ST-Line 5dr	127	51.4	1,250	4.36	2.01	21,290	92	82	72	71	8,804	49,574
Volkswagen Polo: 1.0 TSI 95 SE 5dr	105	61.4	1,069	4.05	1.96	16,775	96	85	76	59	18,398	44,050
Mercedes-Benz A Class A180d: Sport Executive 5dr Auto	103	67.3	1,425	4.3	2.02	26,585	93	81	67	86	4,589	42,862
Mini Hatchback: 1.5 Cooper 5dr	109	60.1	1,145	3.98	1.93	16,615	79	73	66	56	17,447	40,005
Vauxhall Astra: 1.5 Turbo D 105 SRi 5dr	90	64.2	1,403	4.37	2.04	22,730	86	84	83	75	3,419	30,280
Mercedes-Benz C class: C220d AMG Line 4dr Auto	117	62.8	1,570	4.68	2.02	35,740	89	79	66	53	4,733	29,579
Toyota Yaris: 1.5 VVT-i Icon Tech 5dr	93	72.3	975	3.95	1.9	16,145	89	81	60	86	10,992	28,388
Weighted Average (All)	111	60	1,231	Safety Average			89	82	70	68	Total	468,780
Weighted Average (Top 3)	115	57	1,199			Worst	A = Adult Occupant					
Weighted Average (Top 6)	114	58	1,218			Best	B = Child Occupant					
** mpg data relates to EC "combined cycle"						Highest	C = Vulnerable Road User					
						Lowest	D = Safety Assist					

Table 2: Top-ten bestselling GEN-Vs in 2018 as compiled from Department for Transport Vehicle Licensing statistics, Table VEH0160 (updated 19/12/2019). Additional vehicle-specific data courtesy BBC Top Gear online vehicle reviews.

[1] This does not include the Fiesta Active, which has been designated as an SUV crossover.

[2] This does not include the e-golf or the golf GTE (hybrid).

Whilst statistics like this might well, on the face of it, seem to corroborate my worry about the environmental damage being inflicted by the British car buyers who've chosen an SUV in preference to a GEN-V, they actually mean very little unless we can give them some meaning or relevance. Of what concern is it that SUVs, on average, emit 32 g/km more CO_2 than a GEN-V? Acting on advice contained in a report from the Committee for Climate Change (CCC) in May 2019,[1] and influenced too, no doubt, by the climate change protests here and across the world, the UK government agreed to adopt a 2050 target of net-zero GHGs; which, of course, also means a net-zero target for the GHG most abundantly produced by the transport and energy requirements of industrial society: Carbon Dioxide – CO_2. In June 2019, legislation was passed which made the target a binding, legal requirement; and this makes it the one we should all be focussing on if we are serious about supporting our national response to the global climate emergency. Is the target achievable? The CCC is in no doubt that the task is a daunting one and will require each of us to play our part. The following extract is taken from the section on its website which examines the UK's progress to reduce carbon emissions:

Reaching net-zero emissions requires an annual rate of emissions reduction (15 Mt CO_2e per year,[2] 3% of 2018 emissions) that is 50% higher than under the UK's previous 2050 target and 30% higher than achieved on average since 1990. ***This is an indication of how substantial the step up in action must be to cut emissions in every sector.****[3] (My emphasis)

---

[1] Committee on Climate Change website. Publications page. "Net Zero – the UK's contribution to stopping global warming": www.theccc.org.uk/publication/net-zero-the-uks-contribution-to-stopping-global-warming

[2] The little e in CO_2e stands for equivalent or equivalence. Methane embedded underground, by way of example, is 34 times more potent as a GHG than CO_2 is. A 1-tonne reduction of methane emissions would be equivalent to a 34-tonne reduction of CO_2 emissions (i.e.1 tonne of methane = 34 tonnes of CO_2e).

[3] Committee on Climate Change website. UK action on climate change page. "Reaching net zero in the UK": www.theccc.org.uk/uk-action-on-climate-change/reaching-net-zero-in-the-uk

With this urgent analysis from the CCC in mind, one way I can present the SUV and GEN-V emissions statistics in a meaningful way is to assess their implications in relation to our national climate change legislation.[1] Suppose, for a moment, that in 2019 there hadn't been any non-electric SUVs available in the car showrooms; suppose their sale had – as a totally hypothetical flight of extreme fancy – been embargoed for the year: put simply, this would have meant that customers had no choice other than to buy a GEN-V in place of each of the 967,966 non-electric SUVs they would otherwise have done. Then, supposing that the CO_2 emissions from *each* of these non-available SUVs is given by the weighted average of all the 10 SUVs in table 1 (143 g/km) and the emissions from each of the GEN-Vs bought as alternatives is taken from table 2 in the same way (111 g/km), the consequence is a CO_2 saving of 32 g/km for 967,966 vehicles driven on GB roads.[2] Based on a driving average of 7,600 miles each year *per car* (12,231 km),[3] this means the total saving for each year after 2019 can be calculated as 378,854,149 kg – about .38 Mt – of CO_2: that's about 2.5% of the total annual reduction which is needed.[4] To me, this seems highly significant in the light of *how substantial*

---

[1] I'm not, strictly speaking, comparing like-for-like in this analysis. I'm comparing vehicles registered in GB with UK emissions targets. In actual fact UK registrations are higher than GB registrations, as explained in appendix 1. As such, the conclusions I draw from the analysis will **under-represent** the situation. In reality, therefore, the environmental impact of SUV ownership will be worse than I'm presenting it to be. This should be born in mind throughout.

[2] I am trying to illustrate the consequences of choosing to drive a category of vehicle (SUV) that has a higher CO_2 rating (and lower mpg) than an alternative vehicle which could have been chosen. I have therefore chosen the average data from the ten most popular types of GEN-V as representative of the alternative choices available. If Bentley GEN-Vs or Aston Martin GEN-Vs were bought as alternatives, my analysis wouldn't – I accept – be valid. Given, however, that the whole point of the exercise is to try and illustrate the consequences of making choices between high and low emission vehicles, I feel confident my methodology is sound.

[3] Niblefins Motor Insurance website. "Average car mileage UK": https://www.nimblefins.co.uk/average-car-mileage-uk: Note: as mentioned above, the average is *per car.*

[4] One Mt = One million tonnes. One tonne (metric ton) equals 1,000 kg

the step up in action must be. Let me leave my flight of fancy and express it another way. *As a consequence of 967,966 people deciding to buy an SUV rather than a GEN-V in 2019, an additional .38 Mt (378,854,149 kg!) of* CO_2 *will be emitted into the atmosphere annually, representing 2.5% of the amount by which we need to reduce emissions if our agreed target – introduced so that we can avoid an environmental disaster – is to be met.* Please remember that this figure of 2.5% purely reflects the effect of those choices made in 2019 to buy an SUV in preference to a GEN-V; it isn't reflective of the *total* amount of CO_2 emissions coming from the SUVs' exhaust pipes, which is a much higher percentage of the annual reduction we need to make – as we shall soon see.

Suppose that the CO_2 differential between SUVs and GEN-Vs is calculated from weighted average for the top-three vehicles in tables 1 and 2, then it works out to be 34 g/km. Used in relation to additional emissions from SUVs bought in 2019, this would then translate into the slightly higher figure of about 2.7% of the annual savings which we need to make. If we go on to consider the *total* amount of CO_2 emitted from those 967,966 vehicles, which is 1.69 Mt/yr,[1] then this equates to just over 11% of the annual reduction needed.

So far, of course, I've only been considering the emissions' impact in subsequent years of the SUVs bought in 2019. Let's again use the weighted average for all the ten vehicles in each of tables 1 and 2 and then consider the emissions' impact that *all* SUVs which are currently licensed as being on-the-road will already have started to make. At the end of 2018 there were 5,377,433 licensed **non-electric** SUVs. This increased to 6,147,016 at the end of 2019 as we've already footnoted on page 28. Adjusting accordingly, we can take the number of **these** SUVs using the roads throughout 2019 to have been 5,762,224. The amount of additional CO_2

---

[1] 967,966 (vehicles) x 143 (Co_2 – g/km) x 12,231 (average mileage – km/yr)

emissions which will have come from them, compared to those from an equivalent number of GEN-Vs, works out to about 2.26 Mt/yr,[1] which is 15% of the annual national savings we need to make. *In terms of the collective emissions **total**, these SUVs will have emitted a full 10.08 Mt of* CO_2 *during 2019: that's 67% of the annual reduction needed.* The whole basket of greenhouse gases includes many others such as methane and nitrous oxide from agricultural activities and waste management. Were we to consider annual CO_2 emissions *alone*, then – according to the latest information at the time of writing from the Department for Business, Energy and Industrial Strategy (BEIS) – the 2019 total was 351.5 Mt.[2] This means that the SUVs on our roads will have contributed nearly 2.9% of the total – that's 2.9% of **all** the UK CO_2 emissions coming from transport, heating, industry, business, retail, agriculture and waste management: in 2019, *2.9% of ALL these emissions were attributable to SUV usage alone.*

Because the numbers relating to national emissions are so huge, trying to get a sense of what it all means can sometimes be quite bewildering and difficult to compute mentally. But we all have at least some kind of intuitive understanding about the amount of energy we use to heat our homes each year; we have a sense of what it takes to keep our house or flat comfortably warm. For the "average" home, there will be about 2,700 kg of CO_2 released into the atmosphere each year as a result of its heating requirement: the household's heating carbon footprint.[3] The *extra* CO_2 which will be released into the atmosphere each year from those who, in 2019, made a choice to buy an SUV rather than a GEN-V will

---

[1] See footnote 4 on page 54
[2] BEIS download. "2019 UK Provisional Greenhouse Gas Emissions": https://assets.publishing.service.gov.uk/government/uploads/system/uploads/attachment_data/file/875482/2019_UK_greenhouse_gas_emissions_provisional_figures_statistical_summary.pdf
[3] Energy Saving Trust Website: "Significant changes are coming to the UK heating market": https://energysavingtrust.org.uk/blog/significant-changes-are-coming-uk-heating-market#:~:text=Energy%20Catapult%20Analysis%20shows%20that,to%20692%20kg%20CO2%20annually.

therefore be equivalent to the heating carbon footprint of 140,316 homes. The *extra* CO_2 emitted from *all* the SUVs which used our roads throughout 2019 is equivalent to the heating carbon footprint of 835,291 homes. And, finally, the *total* amount of CO_2 emitted from all the SUVs which used our roads throughout 2019 is equivalent to the annual heating carbon footprint of – wait for it – over 3.7 million homes: 3,732,711 to be precise; or nearly 4 million homes in round numbers.

It's crystal clear, then, that SUV ownership in the UK has been nothing if not extremely unhelpful for the national attempt to reduce climate-damaging emissions. And these are just the "tailgate" – exhaust pipe – CO_2 emissions from vehicles. We also need to consider the "upstream" CO_2 emissions that come from oil extraction and refining. And whilst at it, what about the embedded upstream CO_2 emissions which come from vehicle manufacture and maintenance; not to mention road construction and repair? Even though the incremental difference between the impact of an SUV and a GEN-V on road surfaces must be so small as to be virtually unmeasurable, it's there all the same; which means that there must also be a slight difference in the associated upstream emissions. Worry not, however, because drilling down to quite such specific differential detail isn't something which will be feasible – nor particularly useful – here and now. Having acknowledged road construction and repair to be an element of a vehicle's total lifetime carbon footprint that shouldn't be overlooked, as it often is, I shall leave the complex mathematics required to quantify the relationship between specific variables – e.g. vehicle numbers and size – and the frequency that road surfaces need to renewed in the hands of civil engineers.

I need to admit that the topic of upstream emissions from oil extraction and supply has been one of the more complex and difficult aspects of my research. I wanted to be sure that I left no stone unturned, but I had no idea just how heavy some of those stones were going to be. Trying to determine the carbon footprint of the oil industry was one such stone-stoning venture that might well be considered by some to have been foolish-if-well-intentioned. My quest often led me up informational dead ends. I found, for example, an interesting briefing article from Transport & Environment whose title initially looked promising, as did the opening paragraph:

Measuring the carbon footprint of petrol and diesel

In 2009, under the terms of article 7a of the Fuel Quality Directive (FQD), the EU committed to reduce the carbon footprint of transport fuels by 6% by 2020. The carbon footprint consists of emissions that occur during the extraction, processing, production and transport of the petrol and diesel sold in the EU market.[1]

The briefing went on to explain that in order to establish a correct basis from which the required reduction of transport fuel's carbon footprint could be effectively measured – a basis which took variations of carbon-intensity from different production methods into account – the European Commission had proposed asking fuel suppliers to provide information about their supply sources. The object of the whole exercise had been to introduce a system of rewards favouring the supply of transport fuel obtained from cleaner-than-average sources. I suppose, however, that the response which the commission received was only to have been expected:

The oil industry have argued vigorously against these provisions maintaining, among other things, that establishing a chain of custody for its products would lead to unjustified reporting costs and administrative burdens.

Collecting *detailed* information proved to be as difficult for me as it was for the European Commission. Most of the powerful

---

[1] Transport & Environment briefing download. "Measuring the carbon footprint of petrol and diesel": www.transportenvironment.org/sites/te/files/media/2012_04_FQD_report_summary_final_1.pdf

companies involved are reluctant to give too much away, and the requisite facts and figures haven't been uploaded to the Internet – so far as I was able to establish – in the form of comprehensive official reports, only in the form of disparate academic-research papers. Thankfully, however, I managed to find several NGO sources which provided sufficient information for me to use in *summary* form. One of these sources was CarbonIndependent, which has calculated that the *total* amount of CO_2 attributable to vehicle use, inclusive of upstream emissions, is about 32% higher than the tailgate figure.[1] This includes energy used in oil extraction; energy used in oil refining; construction of cars and maintenance; and construction of roads and maintenance.[2] On this basis, CarbonIndependent has calculated that, overall, there will be 14.3 kg of CO_2 emitted for every gallon of fuel which a vehicle uses. The carbonindependent.org website has published a very helpful little guide which gives a visual indication of what this means for different types of vehicles. I have reproduced it as Table 3 below, together with the original explanatory notes.

Size	Average mpg	gCO_2 per mile*
Small, medium, large, city and estate cars	52	280
MPVs and small & medium SUVs	46	310
Sports cars and large SUVs	35	410

*calculated from mpg and CO_2 emissions of 14.3 kg per gallon
Note: Fuel use data has been taken from the *Which?* magazine *Car Guide*[3]. These are measured values under real world conditions rather than the manufacturer's published figures under ideal conditions. The published values have been grouped and averaged as above.

Table 3: Relationship between vehicle size, average mpg and total upstream CO_2 emissions.

---

[1]   CarbonIndependent.org website. "Emissions from cars": www.carbonindependent.org/17.html
[2]   So at least I haven't overlooked the road building & repair aspect of a vehicle's carbon footprint altogether.
[3]   Which magazine (2019) *Car Guide 2019/20* **www.which.co.uk**

If what I've already said about the impact of SUVs hasn't been sufficient, then this table clearly shows that SUVs are even more inefficient than we supposed them to be when *tailgate* CO_2 was used as the basis for evaluation. The information from Table 3 also enables us to perform some honest, mathematical jiggery-pokery to produce a formula for calculating total emissions *per km* – which, given its widespread use in the UK, is a more familiar yardstick than *per mile* is. If we take a vehicle's emissions' figure (CO_2 in g/km) to be X, then the following allows us to calculate it: X = 8,885/mpg. By way of illustration: if a vehicle's fuel economy is 46 mpg, then the CO_2 emissions – X – will be 193 g/km.

Casting our minds back just a bit, we considered some examples showing the impact of an SUV in relation to our UK annual target for reducing CO_2 emissions. Most of these examples were based on the weighted average for SUV emissions of 143 grams of CO_2 per kilometre (table 1). Given that the corresponding average for fuel economy was 48 mpg, we can now use the our X = 8,885/mpg formula to establish that the *actual* CO_2 emissions, allowing for oil extraction, car manufacture etc., should be 185 g/km.[1] Likewise, the actual CO_2 emissions for the "average" GEN-V will rise from 111 to 148 g/km. The gap between the two – i.e. the emissions impact of driving an SUV in preference to a GEN-V – rises from 32 to 37 g/km, an increase of 5 g/km or about 15%. This is less, possibly, than might have been expected, but it is nonetheless clearly significant. It leads to the conclusion that after an upward adjustment has been made which factors in upstream CO_2 emissions for *both* SUVs and GEN-Vs, driving the former is shown to be even worse for the environment compared to the latter than we had previously supposed. I don't, however, want to reinforce this by providing another litany of statistics illustrating

---

[1] This is 1.29% higher than the tailgate figure, very slightly less than the 1.32% suggested by CarbonIndependent. I have traced this small inconsistency back to (i) rounding up/down of averages, and (ii) the source data methodology for reporting a vehicle's emissions.

the effect on our national emissions-reduction target. This can easily be done, if wanted, by recalculating the examples I provided earlier in the chapter using the revised figures above.

The significance of including upstream emissions in a vehicle's carbon footprint is best appreciated, possibly, not so much in how it strengthens the environmental case against SUVs as in how it sends an alarm call to *all* of us about our use of petrol and diesel vehicles. *Warning: our impact on the environment is about 32% worse than we generally suppose it to be.* There are many variables to be included in the calculation of upstream emissions, of course, such as how the crude oil is extracted at source: tar sands oil production, for example, is considered to be 23% more carbon intensive than conventional crude oil extraction.[1] I'm uncertain of the extent to which this been accounted for in the generic upstream-emissions corrective provided by CarbonIndependent. Its corrective has also assumed a constant manufacturing energy-used figure for each vehicle, whereas there will always be variables associated with the amount of steel used in the bodywork and rubber used in the tyres, to take two examples alone. The best we can do *here* is stick with the 32 per-cent-extra figure, whilst bearing in mind that more specific data relating to the source of fuel used, the type of fuel, and vehicle size will lead to variations. These will only be slight when factored into the overall picture, and tailgate emissions will always comprise the largest single element.

Another consideration in the context of our national GHG targets is that many cars we buy are manufactured abroad. In consequence, some of the CO_2 emissions included in the upstream calculation for British vehicles are actually being generated away from our shores; and this raises the question about whether or not they should be included in the calculation. To a certain extent, the same questions can be asked for emissions from oil extraction:

---

[1] I will be looking at tar sands oil production in the next chapter.

some of the emissions themselves – in spite of our North Sea operations – enter the skies above those foreign countries that supply us with oil. None of this is to suggest that these emissions should be ignored, far from it. The only point I'm making is that when we look at emissions in the context of our own *national* targets, as I have done earlier on, then there are additional complications to be considered if we use the total rather than the tailgate figures. None of this changes the alarming disparity between the emissions from an SUV and from a GEN-V. What it does do is send out an additional warning that *none* of us car drivers should be complacent about our impact on the environment, either at home or across the globe.

Before moving on from the subject of emissions to the one of fossil fuel production, I would like to make some comments – *entirely* in parenthesis – which have been prompted by my delving a bit more deeply into reports from Transport & Environment (T&E). My attention was drawn to a press release from March 27th. 2020, which ran:

EU car lobby's renewed attack on cars CO_2 targets – on the back of Covid-19.[1]

Firstly, to set the context:

The car CO_2 law is the primary EU-wide policy to reduce the increasing climate impact of cars, which account for 14% of the EU's overall greenhouse gas emissions and 70% of EU road transport emissions. The first meaningful target, after years of growing CO_2 emissions and a lack of electric car models on the market, kicked in on the 1st of January 2020: 95% of all new passenger car sales EU-wide have to be at or below the average

---

[1] Transport & Environment website. Press Releases: www.transportenvironment. org/press/eu-car-lobby%E2%80%99s-renewed-attack-cars-co2-targets-back-covid-19

targets of 95g CO_2 per km. The target then applies to 100% sales in 2021

Whilst, on the face of it, this would seem to infer the immediate demise of the petrol/diesel SUV (whose emissions are well above this figure), it's not that simple – alas. The targets apply to "fleet sales", which means that emissions' quotas are effectively spread out and averaged across a whole range of sale models. Even so, as we saw on page 30 in respect of falling diesel sales, many manufacturers have apparently been objecting to these targets and offering excuses for why they cannot be met. In its March press release, T&E reported that some manufacturers were also complaining that, because of falling sales caused by the pandemic, the targets are going to be distorted and are therefore unfair and unachievable. According to T&E, however, the logic behind their arguments doesn't bear scrutiny and it therefore dismisses them. In the course of explaining their reasons, T&E makes a very pertinent observation; namely, *that carmaker's fleet emissions have been rising over the past decade as a direct result of pushing SUV sales to increase their profit margins.* I'll take that to be a succinct endorsement of the arguments I've been advancing about the adverse relationship between SUVs and CO_2 emissions! The escalation of SUV sales is authoritatively recognized by T&E as having led to an increase in the total amount of CO_2 emissions from all the cars on our roads when this total should, ideally, be falling.

Chapter Five

Raping the Earth for Oil

The title I've given to this chapter may seem a bit over dramatic. It might also seem unpleasant: it's meant to be. I don't think of myself as a radical person and I've certainly got some footholds in the conventions of the capitalistic Western world. These aren't solid enough to make me suppose I'll be the amongst the first to the gallows come the anti-establishment revolution, but I'll be watching anxiously for where the execution demarcation line is drawn. Hopefully, I'll manage to duck beneath the zealots' radar. If there's one issue which is guaranteed to arouse me from my reactionary stupor and make me become an enraged tree-hugger, however, it's the collective blind eye being shown to how the oil industry produces the fuel that goes into our cars. Where do all the trillions of gallons of the stuff come from? Okay, it's undeniably true that more and more governments are setting dates for the mandatory switch to electric vehicles, and the use of energy from renewable sources is growing apace; so the glory days of oil will eventually be consigned to history. But this remains certain: the oil industry isn't going to go quietly and seems bent on ever more destruction as it breathes its last. Whilst the demand for black gold remains, we can be sure that ways will be found to supply us with it, no matter – so it seems – what the cost. And the rising demand for SUVs over the past ten years or so has demonstrated a callous indifference towards the environmental aspect of that cost.

I don't really need to put on too much of a statistical-gymnastics exhibition to quantify the problem. But here are some calculations to get us started. Utilizing the average mpg figures in tables 1 and 2, and using the 7,600-mile annual average per UK car already referred to,[1] it can be established that an additional 31.67 imperial gallons of fuel will be needed annually for each SUV bought in preference to a GEN-V. For all the 967,966 **non-electric** SUVs bought in 2019, this equates to over 30.6 million gallons of fuel annually.[2] Intuitively, we can immediately recognize that this is a vast amount; it's getting on for enough to fill about 4,000 of the larger road-haulage fuel tankers that we see on UK roads.[3] *Four thousand tankers each year to get all the extra fuel required by the 2019 cohort of SUV buyers to the pumps!* I could attempt a detailed calculation of how much extra fuel these tankers themselves will use, not to mention their CO_2 emissions; but I'm not going to. Anyone who is serious about mapping all the dots delineating their motoring carbon footprint, however, needs to keep knock-on impacts such as this in mind. Suppose, just as little more than a hunch (and one that veers on the lower side to boot), the average *return* journey a tanker makes from refinery to filling station across the country is 50 miles, then our four thousand tankers will collectively travel 200,000 miles each year: it's a nice tidy amount to work with, although I suspect it could easily be twice that amount. Each of these tankers, fully laden on the outward leg of their journey and empty on the return one, will have an average fuel economy in the region of 10 mpg; and that's far more than just guess work. We end up with total diesel usage of about 20,000 gallons a year, and possibly as much as 40,000. I've already acknowledged that this isn't the correct way to make a detailed calculation of the extra road-haulage miles required to deliver the additional SUV fuel: it's a simplification that I strongly suspect leads to an underestimation. Even so, there is no sleight of mathematical hand here, no attempt to conveniently massage the figures; this is legitimate illustration of the hard fuel-related reality that the SUV craze has led to.

---

[1] See footnote 3 on page 54
[2] 30,652,256 gallons
[3] 3,880 road-haulage tankers, assuming tanker size of 7,900 gallons

I'll say no more about the fuel used by the road tankers, but I'd like to provide some further illustrations in the context of crude oil extraction and delivery. To do so, I will need to know the mix of diesel and petrol vehicles[1] within the SUV totals I'll be using as this will affect the calculation for the amount of crude oil needed to supply 30.6 million gallons of refined fuel to the filling stations: one barrel of crude oil[2] will produce 16 imperial gallons of petrol but only 10 imperial gallons of diesel.[3] According to the statista website, the proportional mix for non-electric UK car sales during 2019 was about 30% diesel and 70% petrol.[4] Given that SUVs constituted a large proportion of total car sales, about 42%, we can reasonably assume that this general proportional mix will be roughly replicated within SUV sales themselves.[5] As such, we can use the ratio of one barrel of crude oil to 14.2 gallons of refined fuel. If there is any error in this figure, then it won't be of too much importance as the illustrations I intend to make are themselves general ones.

Putting everything into a number cruncher, what comes out the other side tells us that 2,158,609 barrels of crude oil will be needed to provide enough fuel for the *additional* annual requirements of those who chose to buy an SUV in 2019. I've always found it a bit hard trying to work out what such huge quantities of

---

[1] Allowance for hybrid vehicles is accounted for in the average fuel economy figures which are being used.
[2] 1 barrel of oil = 42 US gallons or 35 imperial gallons. Unless specified otherwise, "gallons" will refer to imperial gallons.
[3] US Energy Information Administration website. FAQs: www.eia.gov/tools/faqs/faq.php?id=327&t=9
[4] Statista website. "Passenger car registrations in the UK between 2016 and 2020, by fuel type": https://www.statista.com/statistics/299031/fuel-types-of-new-cars-registered-in-the-united-kingdom
[5] It's highly unlikely that sales of petrol SUVs would be more than 70%. If, as is more likely, sales were LESS than 70%, then this will mean the need to use a figure of less than 14.2 gallons of refined fuel in our calculations. In turn, this means that the number of barrels of crude oil needed will increase: my illustrations will be understating the amount of crude oil required, not overstating it.

oil actually mean. It might be helpful, therefore, to know that the largest oil supertankers on the oceans today are capable of carrying just over two million barrels of crude oil. *So, each year we shall need the oil carried by about one whole supertanker just to satisfy the **additional** fuel requirements of those British people who, in 2019, decided to buy SUVs in preference to GEN-Vs.* If that doesn't quite sink in, then please also consider some further information about supertankers. The M.V Arcturus Voyager, an American vessel, is 335 metres long; that's nearly three-and-a-half football pitches. Its cargo of 2.2 million barrels would fill getting on for 10,000 of the larger fuel tankers which we see on British roads.[1] It's a phenomenal amount of vanity oil: the oil required just to accommodate those who, in a single year, decided to buy a car which was fashionably oversized.

There are other ways of illustrating the matter. The UK currently consumes 1,583,896 barrels of oil each day.[2] This means that the additional fuel requirement of the 2019 SUV-buyers equates to about 1.4 days of our annual requirement. Or: as a nation we produce about one million barrels of North Sea oil each day;[3] so it follows that the aforesaid SUV drivers require the equivalent of over two days of our national oil production just to satisfy their extra fuel requirement. And given that their *total* annual fuel requirement will be in the order of 153.2 million gallons at the filling station, about 10.8 million barrels of crude oil will be needed: nearly five super-tankers' worth of the stuff – enough to fill nearly 50,000 road-haulage tankers. The volumes are dumbfounding, are they not?

---

[1] 9,738 road-haulage tankers, assuming tanker size of 7,900 gallons.
[2] worldometer website. United Kingdom Oil: www.worldometers.info/oil/uk-oil
[3] 1,083,928 in 2016 (source as footnote 2 above).

A supertanker in dock. Photo from Dreamstime.com under free licence.

The oil carried by one or more of these supertankers will be needed each year simply to supply enough extra oil to accommodate the choice of those who bought an SUV in 2019 rather than a GEN-V. Up to six of these huge vessels were needed in 2019 to carry the additional oil required by all the SUV drivers on British roads.

As if I haven't already bamboozled you – and possibly bored you – sufficiently with these facts and figures, then please allow me to take it all one stage further before I allow some space to draw breath. Taking *all* the non-electric SUVs on the British roads throughout 2019,[1] our number cruncher[2] informs us that there was a requirement of 12.8 million barrels of oil needed *over and above* what would have been required were all these people to have driven a GEN-V[3] – that's roughly equivalent to the amount of oil that can be carried by about 6 super tankers – about 60,000 road-haulage tankers. It also equates to about 12 days of UK oil production. This number is, of course, continuously increasing. The 6,147,016 non-electric SUV drivers on the road

---

[1] Which, if you remember, was calculated to be 5,762,224 during 2019.
[2] In reality, an Excel Spreadsheet.
[3] I would like to remind my readers at this point of the all-important footnote 2 on page 54.

at the end of 2019 will need an extra 13.7 million barrels of crude oil during 2020, and that doesn't take any account of the oil demand created by all those extra SUVs which will be bought and used throughout the year. Without further comment of any kind, I'll conclude with the number of crude oil barrels which were needed to supply sufficient fuel at the filling stations for the SUVs which used British roads in 2019: just over 64 million, enough to fill about 29 super-tankers.

I haven't – intentionally – made reference to the international situation, to the number of SUVs which are being bought each year across the world. This is for the simple reason that I feel it lies beyond my scope. If, however, it's possible to make that leap of imagination and begin to consider what all this means when applied to the world stage, then perhaps some will wish to reconsider their vehicle choice. Although, by my own confession, I've been very slow in developing what I might call a socio-political consciousness, I have nonetheless been aware from childhood that our dependence on oil is unsustainable. Like most, I've looked up at the sky and wondered where the universe ends, or how there can possibly be any ending when we can't conceptualize what lies beyond. As with time, of course, the concept of there being any given beginning or ending just scrambles our brains as surely as an overloaded home computer in need of a reboot. It's only in recent years since being exposed to professor Stephen Hawking's concept of space-time[1] that I've come remotely close to understanding the relevance, if any, of finite terms when used in an astrophysical context. I was, however, able to understand the pertinence of using finite terms in relation to oil supply from a very early age, infinite though we may treat it. I've often stood on the top of a motorway bridge and looked at the constant flow of vehicles in either direction for as far as the eye can see; and then I've thought that this is just one snapshot in time of what's going on ceaselessly from thousands of

---

[1] Which I can only claim to have *partially* understood.

other viewpoints across the UK, and possibly thousands of millions of viewpoints across the world – and, if you like, I've marvelled. I've marvelled no less than I've marvelled looking out across the night sky at the stars. I've marvelled at the apparent incomprehensibility of it all; the incomprehensibility of how such vast amounts of fuel can be produced, delivered, and used up day after endless day; the incomprehensibility of it, that is, to our normal, everyday powers of comprehension: the quantities involved are mind-boggling. Often, when faced with a challenge to our intellectual imagination, we consign the issue to storage somewhere in our brains, possibly to be revisited at some point, and get on with life. But the question of oil's finitude remains. How can its ceaseless cycle of production and supply be sustained? It can't be! Unlike the universe, whose beginning and end is ultimately unknowable (even to those striving to find a unified scientific model), there *has* to be an end to oil, however many imaginative and destructive ways we might deploy to extract every last drop of it. And isn't to do so wrong in itself? Aren't our current attempts coming close to doing just that; like wringing out a wet cloth till the last drop has been expunged? What right have we to do such a thing to a world in which we have no lasting ownership claims, if we could only allow ourselves to think about ownership beyond the Western legal convention: a piece of paper or other certificate of provenance that decrees entitlement, enforceable by law; with law being nothing more in the universal framework than that which can be upheld by the exercise of power. But now I *am* starting to sound radical and have maybe left one or two behind. Perhaps the Patek Phillipe watch advert begins to point us, unintentionally, in the right direction: the idea that we never really own something but look after it for the future generations. As such, we are custodians of all around us, not owners and masters. If we end up bleeding the world dry of something – *anything* – we consider precious, how can we metaphorically look future generations in the eye and try to maintain we discharged our custodial duties honourable? Won't they mock us and say that we were no better than thieves or rapists? Or stupendously short-sighted and selfish at best?

I remember being interviewed for a job back in 1975 in what was then the DHSS.[1] The department queen, as she called herself,[2] asked me what my thoughts were on the oil crisis; what I thought would happen when oil ran out. I was unprepared! I didn't really see what it had to do with social security benefits, but I remained unfazed. "I think they'll have discovered something else by then," I answered blithely. I'd have been hard pressed to say who "they" were if asked; but I wasn't. Exactly who *are* they though? There seem to a lot of them about. All those people, presumably, who we believe are responsible for doing something which we haven't really thought about too much ourselves. Anyhow, I got the job. I guess I demonstrated that I wouldn't be too much a troublemaker; not like an office friend who crossed out DHSS on one of his buff files and gave it some colour by writing in bold pen, "Department for Stealth and Social Insubordination". He didn't last long after that!

The much-feared oil famine never really came; more and more reserves were discovered and exploited. Peak oil[3] seems to be an ever-receding apex: like the rainbow's end, it recedes as you move towards it. We know, however, just how much damage is being inflicted on the planet by burning fossil fuel. That's to say, the majority of dispassionate people do; and it's why the UK government has itself declared a climate emergency. There remain some in the pocket of the oil industry who wilfully dissent, and there are other geological-science flat-earthers and fossil fuel ostriches who, for reasons best known to themselves, either beg to differ or bury their heads in the sand. I must try harder not to quite so rude about them! For now, I'll simply take it as read that we're all singing from the same climate-emergency hymn-sheet and move on. I've already made the direct connection between SUV

---

[1] Department for Health and Social Security.
[2] She was actually called Pauline, and I can still picture her. She was large in every sense of the word and ruled over us more as an empress than a queen. She was a lovely lady who was very kind to me, and I was inordinately fond of her.
[3] The time when maximum oil extraction is reached, and after which extraction goes into terminal decline.

emissions and the added burden placed on climate change targets. I now want to offer an explanation of why I, and many many others of course, are so appalled at the prospect of prolonged fossil fuel usage *regardless* of the emissions issue. I am hopeful that the explanation will strengthen my case against SUVs on the grounds that their ubiquity has been prolonging the desperate caterwauling of the oil industry's last lament and deepening the defiance of its continuously extended swansong whilst it refuses to drop down and die.

As oil reserves become increasingly depleted – which they *must* because it takes millions of years for them to be restored from decaying vegetation – opportunities to extract what remains from comparatively shallow underground reservoirs become scarcer. Determined to keep the golden goose laying her not-so-golden eggs, oil companies have begun investing in activities which are increasingly disastrous for the environment – or potentially so. Tar sands operations, exploration of arctic oil reserves, and deep-sea drilling are just three that I shall reference. My attention was first drawn to the nightmarish reality of tar-sand oil extraction in Alberta, Canada, from reading an article called "Scraping Bottom" by Robert Kunzig, which was published in the National Geographic magazine back in March 2009.[1] It's sub-title well summarizes the point I've made about the lengths which companies are prepared to go to so that oil can keep flowing:

Once considered too expensive, as well as too damaging to the land, exploitation of Alberta's oil sands is now a gamble worth billions

Even before I go any further, however, some may already have identified what might seem to be an inconsistency in where I seem to be leading; namely, that the UK doesn't buy its oil from Canada. We aren't, therefore, *directly* contributing to the problems

---

[1]   National Geographic: www.nationalgeographic.com/magazine/2009/03/canadian-oil-sands

associated with this method of oil production. I fully accept that our connection with what's going on requires a willingness to include ourselves within the global oil market. Taken outside of this context, it's easy enough to understand the logic of someone shaking their head and saying, "not *my* problem, guv!" Being able to accept that each of us are contributory to the problem is facilitated by an understanding of the crucial role played by our old economic friends: supply and demand. In the economist's fanciful textbook world, supply of a product will be regulated to demand through the price mechanism; something we've already touched on concerning the market for cars. At the right price, demand and supply will be in equilibrium. In practice, however, the situation with respect to oil is far more complex, more befitting a PhD thesis than a few paragraphs from a run-of-the-mill economics graduate. Suffice for now to say that *provided demand is robust* oil price is heavily influenced by a combination of the political policies of large oil-producing countries and cartels – such as the USA, Russia and OPEC[1] – and speculation in what is known as the oil-futures financial market. By an accident of geological and geographic fate the UK has its own oil-supply industry, albeit that we continue to be a net importer. Germany, purely by way of example, hasn't been so fortunate. Neither country, however, has much control over price: the price of a barrel of benchmark Brent crude is heavily influenced by what is happening to other benchmark prices across the globe. When the global demand for oil weakens, then powerful interests are no longer able to exert the same kind of control and leverage. A major world event such as pandemic, war or financial collapse can result in a sudden and unexpected fall in the demand for oil and a corresponding collapse of price. These, however, are the exceptions rather than the norm. Between collapses, demand is typically restored fairly swiftly and prices recover. Most of the time, then, demand is king; and it's this demand which is fundamentally responsible for creating the right economic conditions for powerful major suppliers to

---

[1] The Organisation of Petroleum Exporting Countries.

regulate supply and command high prices. Like it or not, every one of us is a constituent part of the global-demand-whole; and it's our collective, relentless, international demand for oil which underpins the price levels that have made its extraction from Albertan tar sands economically viable. We aren't able to disassociate ourselves from the whole tarnished and sticky mess just because we don't import Albertan oil ourselves. When I read the National Geographic article back in 2009, I intuitively felt as responsible as *any* other oil consumer – British, Asian, European or North American – even if the direct chain of responsibility might have been harder to articulate.

Robert Kunzig's article described the scale and complexity of operations to extract oil from impregnated sand beside the magnificent Athabasca river, resulting in what has effectively become a colossal expanse of massive open-pit mines. I would like to quote from the article extensively:

Here Syncrude, Canada's largest oil producer, digs bitumen-laced sand from the ground with electric shovels five stories high, then washes the bitumen off the sand with hot water and sometimes caustic soda. Next to the mine, flames flare from the stacks of an "upgrader," which cracks the tarry bitumen and converts it into Syncrude Sweet Blend, a synthetic crude that travels down a pipeline to refineries in Edmonton, Alberta; Ontario, and the United States. Mildred Lake, meanwhile, is now dwarfed by its neighbor, the Mildred Lake Settling Basin, a four-square-mile lake of toxic mine tailings. The sand dike that contains it is by volume one of the largest dams in the world.

Wherever the bitumen layer lies too deep to be strip-mined, the industry melts it "in situ" with copious amounts of steam, so that it can be pumped to the surface. The industry has spent more than $50 billion on construction during the past decade, including some $20 billion in 2008 alone. Before the collapse in oil prices last fall, it was forecasting another $100 billion over the next few years and a doubling of production by 2015, with most of that *oil flowing through new pipelines to the U.S. The economic crisis has put many expansion projects on hold, but it has not diminished the long-term prospects for the oil sands. In mid-November, the International Energy Agency released a report forecasting $120-a-barrel oil in 2030—a price that would more than justify the effort it takes to get oil from oil sands.*

Nowhere on Earth is more earth being moved these days than in the Athabasca Valley. To extract each barrel of oil from a surface mine, the industry must first cut down the forest, then remove an average of two tons of peat and dirt that lie above the oil sands layer, then two tons of the sand itself. It must heat several barrels of water to strip the bitumen from the sand and upgrade it, and afterward it discharges contaminated water into tailings ponds like the one near Mildred Lake. They now cover around 50 square miles. Last April some 500 migrating ducks mistook one of those ponds, at a newer Syncrude mine north of Fort McKay, for a hospitable stopover, landed on its oily surface, and died. The incident stirred international attention—Greenpeace broke into the Syncrude facility and hoisted a banner of a skull over the pipe discharging tailings, along with a sign that read "World's Dirtiest Oil: Stop the Tar Sands."

Getting oil from oil sands is simple but not easy. The giant electric shovels that rule the mines have hardened steel teeth that each weigh a ton, and as those teeth claw into the abrasive black sand 24/7, 365 days a year, they wear down every day or two; a welder then plays dentist to the dinosaurs, giving them new crowns. The dump trucks that rumble around the mine, hauling 400-ton loads from the shovels to a rock crusher, burn 50 gallons of diesel fuel an hour; it takes a forklift to change their tires, which wear out in six months. And every day in the Athabasca Valley, more than a million tons of sand emerges from such crushers and is mixed with more than 200,000 tons of water that must be heated, typically to 175°F, to wash out the gluey bitumen. At the upgraders, the bitumen gets heated again, to about 900°F, and compressed to more than 100 atmospheres—that's what it takes to crack the complex molecules and either subtract carbon or add back the hydrogen the bacteria removed ages ago. That's what it takes to make the light hydrocarbons we need to fill our gas tanks. It takes a stupendous amount of energy. In situ extraction, which is the only way to get at around 80 percent of those 173 billion barrels, can use up to twice as much energy as mining, because it requires so much steam.

In April 2019, another National Geographic article revisited the Alberta tar sands issue with the headline: ***This is the world's most destructive oil operation—and it's growing***

The 175-odd oil sands mining projects are owned by major oil companies from around the world, including Exxon and China's CNOOC. Together, the companies pump out 2.6 million barrels every day, virtually all of which is shipped to U.S. refineries.[1]

No sign then, after a decade of growth, of operations being scaled back. It was the same decade that witnessed the near-exponential growth of SUV sales here in the UK. I've no doubt that many of those

A Google map 3D screenshot showing the Canadian Boreal Forest alongside the magnificent Athabasca river as it flows north. This is how the landscape looked before tar-sand mining destroyed it.

---

[1] National Geographic magazine website. Article by Stephen Leahy: www.nationalgeographic.co.uk/environment/2019/04/worlds-most-destructive-oil-operation-and-its-growing

Another Google map 3D screenshot further south towards Fort McMurray showing the tar sand mining operations together with all the patchwork of trailings ponds. These mines run for hundreds of miles and can be clearly seen on the Google satellite images.

Aerial view of Alberta tar sand operations.
Reproduced with permission from photographer, Peter Essick

Tailings ponds alongside the Athabasca. Many are separated by thin dams, which are prone to breaching. For every barrel of crude tar oil, six to twelve barrels of tailings waste is produced.
Reproduced with permission from photographer, Peter Essick

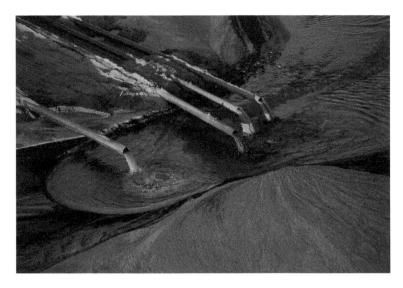

Oil-soaked waste being discharged into a tailings pond.
Reproduced with permission from photographer, Peter Essick

Robotic birds with amplified scaring noises are used to prevent wild birds landing in the tailings lakes, where they get covered in oil and suffer a long slow death. Reproduced with permission from photographer, Peter Essick

An oil-soaked seabird. Reproduced from Fossil Fuel Connections website[1]

---

[1] www.fossilfuelconnections.org/alberta-tar-sands

who bought one of these vehicles haven't even heard of tar sands oil, let alone seen pictures of what's involved. And even if they have, I've already acknowledged that a connection between Canadian oil production and their own vehicle of choice isn't one that most, nor even many, will have necessarily made. If the environmental penny has now dropped, however, and I've spoiled the party, then I can make no apology.

Another feature of the oil industry's continued determination to supply us with the fuel we all hanker – I include myself – is the exploratory risk it is willing to take in its quest to discover as-yet-untapped reserves. The explosion of BP's Deepwater Horizon drilling rig in the Gulf of Mexico back in 2010 is, perhaps, the most infamous example of such risk-taking. The seabed in the area is about 5,000 feet – not far short of one mile; a depth that even BP senior executives have acknowledged to be right at the very frontiers of technological capability. In a 2010 interview for a Der-Spiegel-magazine article about the disaster, then CEO Tony Hayward admitted that:

"The energy industry is clearly working at the frontiers of geology, geography and technology." [1]

It would have been more accurate to have said that the industry was working *beyond* these frontiers. The equipment deployed following the massive explosion on April 20th. 2010 in a remote marine area wasn't of sufficient technological calibre to contain the oil which came gushing from a subterranean reservoir over two and a half miles below the ocean floor where the containing rock was subject to pressures of more than one tonne per square centimetre. The resulting spill was certainly the worst environmental disaster in US history and demonstrated that the industry

---

[1] Der Spiegel magazine. "Does deep sea drilling have a future?" Von Philip Bethqe, Alexander Jung, Nils Klawitter and Renate Nimtz- Koester: www.spiegel.de/international/business/the-risky-hunt-for-the-last-oil-reserves-does-deep-sea-drilling-have-a-future-a-694346.html

had been working *beyond* the frontiers of geology, geography and technological capability. A lake-sized deluge of oil equivalent in volume to over four million barrels was discharged into the sea, forming a slick that Der Spiegel magazine reported as being the size of Luxembourg. Eleven people lost their lives in the disaster, but many more lost their livelihoods as a result of the ensuing marine devastation: the fishing and tourist industries were severely hit. Marine animals took the main impact of the immediate environmental catastrophe, including green, loggerhead, hawksbill and leatherback turtles, gulls, pelicans, roseatte spoonbills, egrets, terns and blue herons. But the full story of the disaster unfolded over several years, including the deaths of migratory ducks and geese, the deaths of numerous baby dolphins during the first birthing season since the spill (2011), and the destruction of coral reefs.

Even though President Obama ordered a six-month moratorium on deep-water drilling, oil companies were soon trying their luck again, this time – allegedly – better equipped to deal with another blow-out. In 2018 President Trump announced a plan that would expand offshore drilling in nearly all US waters, including the Atlantic, Pacific, Gulf of Mexico and even the Arctic, one of the least-developed, ecologically fragile oceans.[1] The North sea, too, finds itself once again in the cross-hairs of exploratory interest. Rowena Mason, writing for the Daily Telegraph in May 2020, has drawn attention to potential defects with a multi-million-pound wellhead-capping device that companies such as ExxonMobil plan to use in the event of a disaster at new drilling sites.[2] With a water depth typically ranging between 100 and 700 feet, the North Sea oil fields were considered to be deep

---

[1]   National Geographic magazine website. "Trump's offshore drilling plan". Elaina Zachos: www.nationalgeographic.com/news/2018/01/trump-administration-announces-offshore-drilling-plans-spd/
[2]   Daily Telegraph website. "North Sea oil leak cap 'may fail' in deep waters": www.telegraph.co.uk/finance/newsbysector/energy/8488465/North-Sea-oil-leak-cap-may-fail-in-deep-waters.html

forty years ago. Areas currently being explored to the west of Shetland, however, are in water depths of up to 6,000 feet. Greenpeace claims that, as happened in the Deepwater Horizon disaster, the oil companies are pushing the technology to unknown limits. The organisation, internationally renowned for its defence of ocean life, is making a legal challenge against the UK government's consent to drilling operations: it – Greenpeace – has serious reservations about the mechanical efficacy of the well cap and hence the ability of oil companies to respond effectively to deep-water accidents.

The investment which companies are making in frontier oil exploration, please remember, is a direct result of it having become financially viable for them to operate in situations that not so long ago would have been prohibitively expensive; and this is all an economic consequence of continued high demand for oil. In the context of my book's subject, therefore, I need to once again highlight that this high demand is itself fuelled, in part at least, by the profligate demand for SUVs. The collective impact that driving SUVs makes on our national oil requirement is by no means inconsiderable – as I've illustrated; so forgive me, please, if one day I find myself incensed enough to forget my manners and frustratedly scrawl "wanker" on the back window of your Range Rover, in my view one of the worst offenders. I've already detailed the phenomenal increase in how many of them there are on the roads, their numbers having increased nearly fourfold over the past ten years to a total of 391,190 at the beginning of 2020. It shouldn't be surprising, therefore, to discover that annual sales have not only matched this level of increase but also exceeded it: there has been a near-fivefold increase over a ten-year period; from 10,324 in 2009 to 51,629 in 2019. Just why are so many more people buying Range Rovers, the second-bestselling SUV? I understand that, for many, it must be to other SUVs what a Rolex is to other watches. But surely that's always been the case? So what's happened in the past ten years to persuade the car-buying public that, at £44,295, the Range Rover Evoque 2.0 HSE has become the must-have car?

It's not only Range Rovers that have enjoyed the surge. Purely from observation in my own neighbourhood (and I'm not quite sure what this says about it), I've noticed a lot more VW Tiguans and Land Rover Discoveries. These came 8th. and 9th. respectively within the 2018 top-ten. Tiguan sales have risen from 7,065 in 2008 to 36,788 in 2019, and Discovery sales from 7,021 to 23,890 during the same period (in 2017 they reached a peak of 34,966). Audi, the Vorsprung Durch Technik company, didn't want to miss the SUV party and therefore launched their "Q" range in 2008. In 2009, the first full-year sales of the beast which is a Q5 were 5,358; by 2019, the number had risen to 12,481. Vorsprung Durch Technik, my ass. Progress Through Technology? At 34–39 mpg for the bestselling TFSI models, I think not. Why – do please help me out, somebody – why has all this happened on our watch when these vehicles have such measly fuel economy and our planet is struggling hard enough as it is to cope with CO_2 suffocation? It certainly doesn't need to cope with further injury from the ravages of an oil industry desperate to squeeze out the remaining oil; an oil industry chasing the profit that's there for the taking whilst demand remains high – a demand buttressed by our car-buying preferences. I don't get it. I honestly and truly don't get it! It's something which does, genuinely, get beneath my skin and explains why I was willing to throw in my lot with Greenpeace on an "action" designed to highlight Cairn Energy's ill-conceived plans to drill for oil in the Arctic.

The year was 2011. The Deepwater Horizon catastrophe less than a year before had been a vivid warning about what happens when 140 million gallons of oil is released into the ocean. Even so, Cairn Energy – a FTSE 100 company launched by former rugby international, Sir Bill Gammell – was pressing ahead with exploratory drilling in the Arctic. Greenpeace UK had been trying to expose the risks involved with such a venture, arguing that they were simply too high – especially when weighed up against the pressing need to reduce the burning of fossil fuel, not increase it. The Greenpeace polar bear – Paula bear – that visited the headquarters of Cairn Energy in Edinburgh may have looked realistic and cute, but for the two activists inside the costume it was hot and demanding work. I can personally testify that they emerged from their polar bear skin at the end of the day dripping with sweat; and all to no avail: the softly-softly approach hadn't worked.

Greenpeace had wanted Cairn Energy to release details of its disaster-mitigation plan, knowing full well that it would have exposed how reckless the drilling operations were. Despite the best efforts of Paula-the-polar-bear, whose visit to Edinburgh had been to create publicity and expose Cairn Energy's Arctic projects as a threat to the survival of such an iconic mammal, the company had repeatedly refused to release the plan. To break the impasse, Greenpeace decided to take direct action; so campaign staff from the London office began recruiting a team of about sixty trained volunteers who would be willing to risk arrest by occupying the Cairn Energy offices in Edinburgh. I was one of the volunteers. After taking part in detailed preparation over a period of several weeks, we made our move as office staff were arriving for work on July 19th. About half of those involved wore polar-bear-head costumes, and the rest of us – their handlers – wore suits. Once inside the building, we padlocked ourselves to the office furniture with reinforced-steel chains and specially constructed – top secret! – lock-on equipment. Non-Violent Direct Actions (NVDAs) such as this, and their resultant publicity, have often bought companies to Greenpeace's negotiating table, with remarkable results in terms of campaign objectives – in this case protecting the Arctic's delicate ecosystem from exploitation and potential destruction.

The Greenpeace "Paula bear" outside Cairn Energy offices in
Edinburgh (2011).

Our polar-bear protest was given considerable media coverage
throughout the day, and the police stayed their hand whilst talks
took place between representatives from Cairn Energy and
Greenpeace. Had these resulted in what the Greenpeace
negotiators considered to be a satisfactory outcome, word would
have been given for us to *collectively* call off and conclude the
NVDA. As the talks progressed, however, separate groups of
activists on different floors of the building were asked by the
action coordinators to unlock themselves and leave; and they were
allowed to do so by the police without arrest. By late afternoon
the talks still hadn't achieved their hoped-for outcome; enough
was enough so far as the police were concerned and a unit of
baseball-hatted response police was drafted in. Only seventeen of
us were left on the top floor and our brief for the situation was to
stay put. The police technicians began the job of cutting us free
with their power tools, although it took them hours to do so. All
of us were arrested and spent the night in police cells. We were
released on bail the following afternoon, charged with taking part
in an activity that was likely to cause fear and alarm.

I didn't acquit myself with flying colours through this short period
of incarceration: it was far worse than I'd imagined possible; not

helped by the extremely unfriendly way in which some of the officers at the station treated us – including a full strip search inside a cold cell. There wasn't even a blanket when the cell door was locked shut for the first time, and the flimsy plastic-coated mattress was still soaking wet from having just been dowsed down. I had to dry it off with toilet paper before I could even sit on it. The contempt some of the officers felt towards us wastrels was evident: that they felt we were wasting *their* time and *public* money was perfectly clear and a few of them actually said as much. I personally felt seriously degraded and it wouldn't be too far from the truth if I said that I hated every moment of the experience. The NVDA, however, ultimately bore fruit. As a consequence of the exposure which it had provided, Cairn Energy's emergency plan was finally published by the Greenland government; and its poorly considered content led to accusations of Cairn Energy being "Arctic Cowboys". The plan effectively conceded that in the aftermath of a spillage huge quantities of oil would remain in the area indefinitely owing to the complexities of any clean-up operations, which would freeze to a halt during the long dark months of the Arctic winter, and beyond. Their fanciful concept of transporting huge sections of oil-impregnated ice to locations where the frozen blocks could be thawed and cleaned left them looking comically ill-prepared to the concerned lay person and expert alike. Friends of the Earth, Scotland, released a wonderful spoof Spaghetti Western video called "Cairn Cowboy Calamity", set to a soundtrack featuring "the Good, the Bad and the Ugly". It's well worth taking a look![1]

I'm not an especially virtuous person and have made many unprincipled decisions that will always be blots in my copy book. But chasing after wealth and riches hasn't been one of my main downfalls: I've preferred to try and find happiness and contentment from who I am rather than what I have; a possible explanation for why happiness has frequently been evasive. In spite of

---

[1]   Cairn Cowboy Calamity. Friends of the Earth Scotland: https://vimeo.com/54610965

this, I *do* notionally understand about the financial motivation which will enable some to ignore whatever obstacles there may be en-route to their hoped-for bounty of greenbacks by the thousand, million, or even billion. Objections from organisations such as Greenpeace or Friends of the Earth must be easy enough to swat away as tiresome arthropodal irritants when all you can think about is the possibility of a massively enlarged balance on your current account. That, I can only suppose, is how those right at the very top of Cairn Energy must have felt with regard to their Arctic drilling plans: they certainly weren't going to be easily thwarted by problematic environmental sensibilities. But maybe our objections added to the existing unease felt by shareholders when the drilling operations didn't seem to be discovering very much. Perhaps the realization that their by-comparison smallish company was in no position to shoulder the $40 billion bill handed to BP following the Deepwater Horizon affair – let alone whatever sum it might escalate to if anything similar happened off Greenland's Arctic coast – helped concentrate the minds of key shareholders sufficiently to make a difference. Who knows? What we *do* know is that the drilling projects were shelved in 2012 and have never resumed. And in November 2011, at the Edinburgh Sherriff Court, Sheriff Roderick MacLeod found one of the Greenpeace activists, Natasha Smith, not guilty of the charges brought against her by the Crown. In his judgement, he said:

I'm not prepared to hold that people who have entered a building dressed in unusual costumes constitutes threatening behaviour.

Nice one, Rod!

Following Natasha's acquittal, the Crown dropped its charges against the rest of us and my Disclosure and Barring Service (DBS) record remained untarnished by criminality. Would I do it again? I don't know! I'd like to think I *would* if it became necessary, but I can't be sure. Perhaps the experience helps explain why I get so impassioned about the absurdity of SUVs. I did something which I thought was right at the time, and I knew all along it was because I felt so strongly about the need to protect our environment against despoilment from oil-extraction operations. The NVDA had a marked effect on me, so happily it seemed to have been worthwhile. But was it? Was it worthwhile when all that oil companies like Cairn Energy are doing, really, is responding to *consumer* demand? Provided there is a profit-motive carrot dangling in front of them and they aren't restrained by law enforcement, isn't it the case that where one oil company has failed another will step in? It's a bit like the international narcotics market, isn't it? One big drugs-bust may represent a battle won and a victory claimed, but the war goes on. The supply of drugs and the demand for them seems to be a continuous self-reinforcing circle; so too with the demand for oil and its supply. The battle won against Cairn Energy was important, but it didn't get anywhere near to solving the problems created by a rampant oil industry; an industry buoyed up the knowledge that demand for its black gold remained vibrant. In the following decade I looked on more or less helplessly as the SUV craze really gathered pace. In my own eyes, it's a craze which has shown a piteous disregard for the welfare of our world. And for what? For some kind of rufty-tufty feel-good experience?

CHAPTER SIX

BRUTALITY

Further on in this chapter I shall take a look at pickup trucks with extended cabs: vehicles which are increasingly used as family SUVs and which never really see the light of a good, honest, hard-day's work on a farm, as a Light Goods Vehicle (The Department of Transport categorize them as LGVs) or as a builder's truck. Before that – and there is a connection which should become apparent – I'd like to make some admittedly subjective comments about the size of conventional SUVs.

Hanging on my study wall is a copy of that well-known, quasi-religious tract we know as "Desiderata". Some consider it to be slushy and sentimental; but I'm not one of them. I was introduced to it, I'll not deny, by listening to the 1972 Les Crane "single" on my little tranny radio, which was more or less constantly tuned and retuned into radio Luxembourg as the signal came and went. Much of Desiderata's advice has been of help to me throughout my adult life, whilst other social, political and religious influences have taken their turn to wax and wane. One verse reads:

"Avoid loud and aggressive persons; they are vexations to the spirit."

If SUVs were people – just as the Reverend Wilbert Awdry's trains are on the Island of Sodor – then I suggest they would be the very same loud and aggressive ones whom the hand behind Desiderata urges us to avoid. Truly! They are vexations to the spirit! I'm not sure I can think of a more apt way to describe them. Perhaps this is best exemplified in those grotesquely large models which have facial-like grills and contours that seem designed to make you feel that they're snarling at you.

A snarling BMW X5 which pulled up in front of me in a
supermarket car park. © John Everett

Their sheer size is aggressive. It could be a BMW X5, an Audi Q5,
a VW Touareg, a Vauxhall Grandland X, a Porsche Macan, or
even one of the ubiquitous Kia Sportages: they're all basically
clones of the same thing and I'll bet many couldn't tell them apart!
Only those fanatics – like me – who notice the differences in
badges, grills, lights and body contours can tell which is which.
It's true that they're attention grabbing; but for all the wrong
reasons. Their very in-your-face-ness is insulting and confronta-
tional. If that's the image you wish to project, then so be it: it's
certainly not one that I find in any way attractive or stylish. At the
risk of repeating myself, I can't deny that there are shades of grey
in all of this. There's a smallish burgundy Mazda CX-3 that is
often parked at the bottom of our road which I almost like, for the
colour I think as much as anything else. I can't say, either, that I
find the Skoda Yeti unattractive: it certainly lives up to Skoda's
former reputation for quirkiness and looking different – Jasper
Carrot would have had a field day with it. At some point, I guess,
the Skoda production team got together and said, "we can't be
having this, we need something which looks like all the other
SUVs." So they booted the Yeti out of production and gave the
world the Kodiaq and the Karoq instead – two for the price of
one. Even with my trained spot-the-SUV-eye, honed to perfection

through my research, I'd be hard pressed to positively identify one of these new models should it bear down on me when I'm driving on the A1M.

To round off this little diatribe about the general appearance of SUVs, especially their size, let's compare and contrast the kerb weights.[1] For our top-ten SUVs from table 2, the average kerb weight was 1,562 kg; compared to the GEN-V average from table 1 of 1,185 kg – a significant difference I'm sure you'll agree. The range between the SUVs was 1,119 kg (Nissan Juke) and a truly hefty 1,954 kg (Land Rover Discovery). 1,954 kg, by the way, is very nearly 2 imperial tons (1.923 tons to be precise). What, may I ask, is a vehicle like that doing in a Tesco car park? The range between the GEN-Vs was 975 kg (Toyota Yaris) and 1,425 kg (Mercedes A180).

If the matter of supermarket car parks has been mentioned a few times, it's because it's one of the places where the impact of an SUV's size most frequently and noticeably imposes itself on everyone else; and if you've been sandwiched between two of them, which you surely *must* have been, you'll understand what I mean. I would personally hate to impose myself on other people in such an annoying way; I'd be constantly feeling that I should leave a note on the affected person's car windscreen to say sorry. I would, genuinely, feel ashamed of my vehicle's size. I can only suppose that owners of large SUVs must have very thick skins; and I'm not meaning to sound offensive or unkind. But they must, mustn't they? What other explanation is there? Do they really not care that their huge vehicle is making life difficult for others? According to Wikipedia (which seems to know everything), the recommended standard parking bay size in the UK is 2.4 metres wide (7.9 ft) by 4.8 metres long (16 ft). The width of SUVs in table 1 varies between 1.98 metres (the Nissan Juke) and 2.17 metres (our old friend, the Land Rover Discovery). These measurements,

---

[1] The kerb weight is without any load in the vehicle: passengers, luggage, work equipment, freight etc.

incidentally, include wing mirrors; which is only right when we're discussing the logistics of trying – or not trying – to park considerately in a supermarket car park. Using the data in tables 1 and 2, some nifty mental arithmetic tells me that when I pull up next to a Discovery in my Golf, I've got slightly over half a metre (.54m) to open my driver's door and squeeze out – OK! I used a calculator to work out the space. And I'm also assuming that we've both managed to park in exactly the middle of our allotted standard-sized space: which SUV drivers *never* do, and I *always* do! Unsurprisingly, I've come very close to causing a disturbance on account of the way in which I've expressed my unrighteous – or, more accurately, *self*-righteous – car park rage on occasions: occasions when Sheriff Roderick MacLeod may well have been justified had he found me guilty of threatening behaviour. But look! At 2.17 m wide, the Discovery is a full .27 m wider than the Toyota Yaris: that's very nearly a foot (10.62 inches), which is massive when it comes to parking. No wonder the Wikipedia article I read also tells us that there has been controversy about the size of parking spaces in recent years.[1] In *my* humble opinion, the controversy shouldn't be about the size of parking spaces so much as the size of the vehicles.

Vehicle length itself isn't normally an issue for most vehicles at the supermarket. Many SUV drivers, however, do seem to have a struggle fitting between the white lines. At 4.59 metres long, the Discovery can only just manage to squeeze itself into its allotted 4.8 metre space. The easiest way to resolve this, I imagine, is to give up trying to; and thus we have the supermarket free for all. My comments might be roguish; but not totally out of order – see below.

---

[1] Wikipedia. Parking Space: https://en.wikipedia.org/wiki/Parking_space

The Supermarket Shuffle © John Everett

In the above photo-montage, I just can't feel that the BMW in the bottom right looks like anything other than what I would call a bus: on the basis of proportions and size, its entitlement to be included within the vehicle class of *car* is nonexistent. What the eye sees, of course, can be conditioned by what it's used to seeing; so nowadays when we see an old Vauxhall Viva, for example, we take a gasp and say "my gosh! Cars were SO small back then!" I used to think the Ford Cortina was a large car, but I'm sure I wouldn't think so if I saw one drive past today. Even allowing for our constantly changing perception of normality, however, I can't stop myself looking at the SUVs above and thinking they look disproportionately big and consquently ungainly; offensive even. I don't think I'm alone. Furtherstill, I find the sense of entitlement represented by driving around in a vehicle which is, quite simply, far too big extremly disquieting: it represents a poke in the eye to the environement and neighbour alike, and it occasionally leads me close to despair.

I've heard it said that many people buy SUVs because they're believed to be safer. I'll grant that crusing down the motorway in one must be, for some, a driver's dream; although, if it was me at the wheel, I'm not sure I'd feel confident of coming out of a brush with a Prestons-of-Potto curtainsider any more intact than I would do had I been in my Golf. Maybe, however, there are other crash scenarios in which an SUV's sheer size *would* afford me the confidence of having additional protection. Maybe! In terms of the average Euro NCAP percentage safety ratings (see tables 1 and 2 in chapter one), the top-ten SUVs *do* show a very marginal safety premium in comparison with the top-ten GEN-Vs across all four categories. The respective average percentages for "adult occupant", "child occupant", "vulnerable road users" and "safety assist" are 92, 84, 71, and 75 for SUVs, and 89, 82, 70, and 68 for GEN-Vs. I've heard concerns for the safety of children in particular being spoken about; but I'm yet to be convinced that it's anything more than a justification for a decision which has been made for other reasons: the average child-occupant-safety score for SUVs is 84, just 2 percentage points higher than the average for GEN-Vs, which is 82. What's more, there are three of the top-selling SUVs which only have a score of 83 for child-occupant safety, and there are four of the top-selling GEN-Vs which have a score in excess of this. Nonetheless, it remains an indisputable fact that the SUVs come out highest for safety overall, if only marginally, and I recognize that this is a perfectly justifiably reason in its own right for buying one; it would be churlish of me not to.

The Mitsubishi L200 can cope with the most rugged terrain.
Photo from shutterstock.com under licence

I can't find any similar justification for buying one of those outlandish, elongated pickup trucks – sometimes known as flat-beds – that are now doubling as SUV alternatives on account of the spacious cabin interior, which has the same comfort level offered by many conventional vehicles and can accommodate five people. To be clear about the kind of vehicle I'm referring to, the picture above shows a Mitsubishi L200 doing the kind of rugged thing it's best at.

Most men and women who identify, or would like to identify, with bloke-culture – the very anithesis of woke-culture – would no doubt like to drive one of these, and I don't doubt there's a little bit of that in many of us: the thought, my Lord, of standing on a corner in Winslow, Arizona and watching some damned pretty girl in a flat-bed Ford slowing down to take a look at you remains such a fine fantasy sight to see for; well, for most of my generation anyway.[1] For those not needing the open flat-bed bit, a secure hard top can be added making it into a kind of gigantic boot. Here's one such L200 in, yes, our local Tesco Extra car park.

Mitsubishi L200 pickup with hard top canopy. © John Everett

---

[1] Those unfamiliar with "Take it Easy" by the Eagles may wonder what on earth I'm jibbering about. Apologies!

It seems as removed from the dusty old battered-about pickups of Mid-West ranchers as I can imagine: if you can visualize the flat-bed which Jake Gyllenhaal's character, Jack Twist, drove in Brokeback Mountain (see picture below), then that's the kind I mean.

The trend for buying luxury pickups is recognized by Carbuyer magazine. In an introduction to their "Best Pickup Trucks" feature – updated in January 2020 – they wrote:[1]

Pickup trucks are increasing in numbers on UK roads these days, but they have a long way to come to match the popularity that they have in North America. That said, we can't seem to get enough of big, tough vehicles these days, with the sales of 4x4s and SUVs also shooting up.

Sales increases have gone hand-in-hand with pickup trucks becoming far easier to live with. Their driving experience has become much more car-like, and in most models the interior quality has gone from cheap and utilitarian to comfortable and luxurious. Muddy maps

1950 Black GMC driven by Jake Gylenhaal in Brokeback Mountain.
Image source not found

---

[1] Carbuyer website. Reviews page. Best pickup trucks: www.carbuyer.co.uk/reviews/recommended/best-pickup-trucks

have been replaced with sat-nav screens and double-cab versions are fitted with four doors and accommodating rear seats, making them as useful on a family holiday as they are on a building site.

There are eight of these pickups sold in the UK. These are:

- Ford Ranger
- Mitsubishi L200
- Nissan Navara
- Toyota Hilux
- Mercedes X-class
- Volkswagen Amarok
- Isuzu D-Max
- SsangYong Musso

The first four of these were all on sale back in 2001, which is the year my DfT registration information goes back to. That year, 9,675 vehicles were sold. By 2010, numbers had increased to 16,876. In recognition of an emerging market, no doubt, VW introduced the Amarok in 2011, and the Isuzu D-Max became available in 2012. Sales of all six continued rising through to 2015, when the total reached 38,785. The Mercedes X-Class and the SsangYong Musson joined the jamboree over the next couple of years, and by 2019 total sales were an astonishing 51,164: that's an increase of 41,489 in the annual sales figures compared to just eighteen years previously. I simply don't believe that the increases can be explained by a corresponding rise in the number of builders, farmers and other tradespeople who have needed and been able to afford a pickup. Quite simply, more and more pickups are being bought for what insurance companies would classify as social, domestic and pleasure usage.

Given that there are far fewer model lines involved than for the SUVs and GEN-Vs I've been analysing, I have been able to make calculations of average CO_2 emissions and fuel economy that I can claim with even greater confidence to be representative of the class as a whole.[1] I analysed information for the top-six bestselling pickup models, which had 48,872 registrations in 2018: 96% of the annual total. The data is reproduced below as table 4. As a weighted average, then, the pickups on British roads emit 192 grams of CO_2 per km and return a fuel efficiency of 38.9 mpg. The figures are in line with what one would probably expect, although they do mask some significant variations. The Ford Ranger, which is the market leader by far,[2] has a CO_2 average across the model range of 209 g/km and a fuel efficiency of 35.7 mpg. By contrast, the Nissan Navara has figures of 172 g/km and 43.6 mpg – easily the best.

Make & model	CO_2 (g/ km)	mpg **	Kerb Weight (kg)	Length (m)	Width (m)	List Price (£)	Euro NCAP Safety (%)				2018 "model" numbers
	Average across range						A	B	C	D	
Ford Ranger	209	35.7	1917	5.36	2.16	33,404	96	86	81	71	15914
Mitsubishi L200	186	39.8	1790	5.28	1.81	25,050	81	84	76	64	9045
Nissan Navara	172	43.6	1991	5.33	2.08	31,360	79	78	78	68	9062
Toyota Hilux	189	39.1	1880	5.33	1.85	26,340	93	82	83	63	6814
Isuzu D-Max	183	40.4	1994	5.29	1.86	20,499	83	67	51	71	4748
VW Amarok	203	36.2	1880	5.25	1.95	36,991	86	64	47	57	3289
Weighted Average (All)	192	38.9	1901	Safety Average			86	77	69	66	48872
** mpg data relates to EC "combined cycle"						Worst	A = Adult Occupant				
						Best	B = Child Occupant				
						Highest	C = Vulnerable Road User				
						Lowest	D = Safety Assist				

Table 4: Top-six bestselling pickups (LGVs) in 2018 as compiled from Department for Transport Vehicle Licensing statistics, Table VEH0160 (updated 19/12/2019). Additional vehicle-specific data courtesy BBC Top Gear online vehicle reviews.

---

[1] A full explanation is given in Appendix 4.
[2] There were 15,914 registrations in 2018. The second bestseller was the Nissan Navara, with 9,062 registrations.

Using the average data for the 2018-registered pickups and apply-ing it to all of the 410,984 licenced vehicles on the road at the end of 2019, I have calculated that the annual amount of CO_2 emis-sions will be about .965 Mt.[1] This equates to about 6.4% of the 15 Mt annual reduction that we need to make in the UK.[2] And if that doesn't strike you as being shameful from just under 411,000 vehicles, let me make some other observations. We already know that the heating carbon footprint for the average UK household is 2,700 kg of CO_2 per year. This means that the CO_2 coming from the exhaust pipes of all the 410,984 pickups on British roads during 2020 will be equivalent to that which is emitted from heating 357,763 homes. As with previous illustrations for SUVs, I haven't included the vehicles which will be bought and driven during 2020, so the actual emissions are going to be higher.

Consider another other way of illustrating the data: the annual amount of CO_2 emitted from heating an average British home, 2,700 kg, and that emitted from driving a pickup truck for a year, 2,350 kg, are roughly of the same order. In other words, each year the "average" pickup will emit nearly as much CO_2 as that which comes from its household's boiler. Now surely there's a thought. And just to round things off, all the pickups on British roads at the end of 2019 will require between 5 and 8 million barrels of oil each year to provide enough fuel for them at the pumps: as many as nearly four supertankers to supply the fuel which will keep them trucking – enough to fill up to about 40,000 road-haulage fuel tankers.

All the comments I've made about the size and brutality of large SUVs apply to pickups, only more so to the nth. degree. Personally, I find them visually oppressive and repulsive. With lengths between 5.25 and 5.36 metres, there's no way one is ever going to fit into a

---

[1] I am again using the average annual mileage figure of 7,600 m/12,231 km (footnote 3 on page 54).
[2] As previously mentioned, I'm **understating** the case by contrasting GB data with UK data. Please see footnote 1 on page 54.

standard parking space: they're not meant to, so I get extra mad when they try. And I play a little game when I'm out and about called *look for any signs of the payload area having been used* – the payload area is the flat-bed bit at the back where rubble, bricks, roofing tiles, general building materials, electrical switchgear, fence posts, cattle feed, or bales of hay are meant to go. The idea of the game is to take a sneaky look inside as you go past and keep a tally of how many you discover where the payload area looks as if it's never been used. When you find yet another one, you can then slowly shake your head, make tut-tut noises, and raise your eyebrows in knowing expressions of judgemental disbelief; although the expressions-bit is an optional extra for those who are as jaundiced and intolerant as I am. It's quite a risky game to play as the owner may well catch you and ask what the hell you think you're up to: they can be very protective of their pickups and are often quite burly-looking bloke-ish blokes. Telling them the truth would lead to offense, so I normally lie shamefacedly and say I'm just generally admiring the vehicle – or something like that. This normally gets the owner brimming with pride and you'll probably be invited to take a look inside the cab. When this has happened to me I've neatly and politely side-stepped the offer by nodding towards a waiting wife. Jeanne usually keeps on the other side of the road and won't have any part of my silly little infantile game, so thank goodness one of us is reasonably sane and willing to think the best of people.

It's not even possible to play the sense-of-safety card to justify pickup ownership, even though that may come as something of a surprise. The averaged percentage safety figures across all four Euro NCAP categories, as shown in table 4 above, are 86, 77, 69, and 66, which compares unfavourably with the averaged top-ten GEN-V percentage safety figures in table 1 of 89, 82, 70 and 68. From all the vehicles whose safety score I've looked at during my research, the VW Amarok – with a percentage score of 64 – is only beaten to the wooden-spoon award for child safety by the little Fiat 500 with a score of 53; and the Amorak's feeble score of 47 for the safety of vulnerable road users is quite frankly disgraceful.

I'm sure it will be a relief to know that the adult-occupant percentage safety score bears up reasonably well across the whole pickup range (I think international vehicle safety legislation may have something to do with it); although with a score of 79, the Nissan Navara is only beaten to bottom, once again, by our little friend the Fiat 500 – which scores 66.

Is there *any* redemption? There most certainly is! I'm sure the utility companies, for example, find pickups invaluable for transporting people and heavy equipment across rugged terrain; and in all weathers too. Quite frankly, they're superb in a wide range of agricultural, industrial and construction settings. I spent three years working on a farm whilst I was trying to support myself through postgraduate education, and I drove tractors out in the fields all year round. The old tractors we drove were open to the elements, without even a basic cab; so it wasn't all fun and games by a long stretch of the imagination: there were many wet, freezing-cold winter days when I'd have loved to be inside the heated cab of, say, a new John Deere with all its mod cons. It's much the same with pickups, I imagine. Leaving Hollywood schmaltz aside, I reckon most normal people needing to use an LGV would choose a modern Ford Ranger in preference to Jake Gyllenhaal's beat-up old flat-bed. I don't begrudge those SSE workers the comfort of their Mitsubishi L200s whilst they drive across wind-and-rain-swept Northumberland moorland to fix some power cables that have come down in the latest storm. Also, the 4x4 traction and payload-area carrying capacity of a pickup fully comes into its own across such terrain; as it does in many other agricultural, construction and commercial settings. And having mentioned my days as farm worker, let me slip in another confessional aside: again, purely by way of anecdotal interest. When I wasn't out in the fields, I also got fairly handy as a mechanic back in the farm's workshop. It was a proud day for me when I pressed the starter button on an old David Brown, which I'd stripped down and rebuilt, and heard the engine come back to life – somewhat hesitantly to begin with. The fact that the crankshaft sheered in two a few weeks later is, however, something best forgotten. It was presumably because I'd replaced the big-end thrust bearings with the oil grooves pointing outwards rather than inwards – but who knows? I never owned up to it!

Although a pickup is undeniably valuable in various work-related and off-road situations, it surely can't be considered justifiable to own one purely for those comparatively few occasions when the British weather makes a journey something of a challenge, or even hazardous? Those who live in remote rural areas, especially isolated dwellings at the end of long or steep lanes, may well need a vehicle they can rely on to cope; but that doesn't necessarily mean a pickup: I'd have recommended a Land Rover Defender in one of their former lives, but not any longer; maybe a Panda 4x4 should do the trick? I read on one manufacturer's website that their pickup is guaranteed to take you through floods of up to 80 cm. I'm impressed; but I can only think of two or maybe three occasions when that would have been useful for me personally. For the past ten years or so I've had to make regular work visits to the Lake District. Getting there normally involves crossing the A66, which is notoriously hazardous on its high sections across the Pennines and is regularly closed in winter on account of snow or high wind. When closed, the only alternative is to try and pick your way through winding lanes that themselves can be even more hazardous. To date, however, I've always managed to get there and back somehow or another, although I came hellish close to defeat in February this year – 2020 – when torrential rain meant that many Lake District roads were impassable. My trusted Golf carried me through floods that must have been up to a foot deep in places. Often, after heavy snowfall, my biggest problem has been getting out of our little estate onto the main roads; but good quality snow tyres have seemingly put paid to all my anxieties. Call me reckless, but I sometimes think there isn't much that my Golf can't tackle with its snowshoes on. Discretion being the better part of valour, however, I *did* turn back last year whilst trying to take Jeanne to work in Darlington: the blizzard was just that bit too fierce and I know when I'm beaten. I think it would have been foolhardy carrying on, even in a Ford Ranger. My point is not to try and deny that 4x4 utility and payload space wouldn't occasionally be useful for most of us; of course it would. I just don't believe that we actually need the overkill of owning a pickup that's designed to tackle the most challenging of off-road conditions; and especially not when we're trying to combat the very climate change that's most likely bringing us the more-frequent storms that are causing problems such as road flooding. The irony is that we don't need more big cars in response to the storms, we need a lot less of them.

CHAPTER SEVEN

ELECTRIC SUVS

Were it not for the Coronavirus pandemic, this year – 2020 – had been looking set to become the one when there was a significant shift in the pattern of vehicle sales in general. Propelled in large part, no doubt, by the need to comply with European legislation on emissions, plug-in hybrid powertrains have been introduced as an option on a significant range of cars, from Minis to the Bentleys. With many models now having an all-electric range of 20 to 30 miles, and some having a price tag that will no longer be considered exorbitant, a certain "buzz" was discernible in the first few months of the year about an anticipated large increase in the sales of Plug-in Hybrid Electric Vehicles (PHEVs).[1] Battery Electric Vehicles – known as BEVs or just EVs[2] – had also looked set to make their mark. Tesla EV sales had shown increases from 4,744 in 2017 to 14,385 in 2019. Another EV, the Nissan Leaf, had been notching up sales of around 5,000 a year since 2015. And with a whole raft of other EV models – including the Mini-e, The Corsa-e, the Peugeot e-208, the e-Golf, and the Audi e-tron – becoming available to

---

[1] Most PHEVs have battery-powered motors fitted to one set of wheels (some have a motor on all four wheels). They also have a conventional petrol or diesel engine to drive the other set of wheels or work alongside the electric motors to power all the wheels. The technology allows the vehicle to be driven with both power sources being used in varying degrees together, or, alternatively, exclusively on electric or petrol/diesel. In all-electric mode, most can be driven for up to around 30 miles, dependant on driving technique and conditions. Once the battery is exhausted, the vehicle can then be driven using the conventional engine. The battery can be recharged at roadside charging points or from a home electricity supply.

[2] BEVs or EVs are driven purely from electric battery power: there is no additional petrol or diesel engine in them.

order, the market looked set for take-off. In October 2019, Seat announced that its Mii Electric would be priced from £19,300, which makes it a genuine contender for consideration by those who have wanted to invest in electric technology but couldn't afford the likes of a Tesla or even a Nissan Leaf.

Because of Covid-19, 2020 may no longer be the electric lift-off year that had been anticipated. The post-pandemic world of motor sales will inevitably look markedly different to what it would have done without the prolonged interruption. Our whole economy and society will look different. Trying to speculate, however, about the likely changes and their duration is somewhat akin to crystal ball gazing and is certainly well beyond my scope here. Whatever happens, though, I don't think they're can be much doubt that sooner or later PHEVs will start selling in far greater numbers than has yet been the case. I suspect it will be tempting for those who buy one, including an SUV model, to feel they've discharged their environmental responsibilities with probity and done their bit for the planet. But PHEVs don't *necessarily* confer environmental benefit. And an SUV fitted with a plug-in hybrid powertrain remains, by definition, an SUV – with the same inherent problems associated with size. In its 2017 review of the Mercedes GLE 550e SUV, Carbuyer magazine acknowledged these issues, if only from the perspective of financial economy.

*Low exhaust emissions are the main point of plug-in hybrid cars, and the 500e's 78g/km CO_2 figure is by far the lowest in the GLE range. This means a far more attractive Benefit-in-Kind (BiK) company-car tax rate than even the entry-level diesel model. If you're in a position to take advantage of this, the GLE 500e makes a sound choice. Its case for private buyers isn't quite so clear-cut. If your daily commute is in urban traffic and is shorter than the GLE's claimed all-electric range of 18.6 miles, you can enjoy petrol-free zero-emissions motoring, but once you leave the city limits you're likely to see fuel economy far more in line with a typical 3.0-litre petrol engine in a heavy SUV. **If you make regular*** *long motorway journeys, a GLE diesel will be far more cost-effective.*[1] (My emphasis)

So there we have it, straight from the automobile-world horse's mouth; not mine. If a PHEV uses its main engine for prolonged periods on, say, long motorway drives, then its *actual* fuel economy will worsen considerably and its *actual* emissions will also increase: the two go hand in hand. As I previously commented in relation to the Bentley Bentayga back in chapter one, the real-world performance data for a vehicle is likely to be considerably different once the car is taken onto the open road beyond the city. *Any* vehicle using plug-in hybrid technology is subject to the same essential criticism, of course. Without wishing to decry the potential benefits of PHEVs, I don't think that the environmental one is *necessarily* quite so clear-cut as it may appear to be; it all depends how the vehicle is used. And I still think that car buyers will be drawn to SUVs for the same status and size reasons they presently are, even if the PHEV option is something of a salve to the conscience. This appears to be confirmed by the next sentence in the Carbuyer review of the GLE SUV that I've just quoted from:

However, the plug-in hybrid's sporty performance is a definite attraction – it's nearly as quick as the range-topping AMG 63 and a whole lot more subtle to look at or to listen to. Like any other GLE, it offers spacious accommodation for five and a big boot.

What of the EV in general and the electric SUV in particular? In spite of the present motor trade uncertainty, there can be little doubt that electric is the way forward and EVs are set to become the norm. On the very day I began writing this section (April 4th. 2020), I also read a report in the Times by Graeme Paton, transport correspondent, under the headline:

---

[1] Carbuyer magazine website. Car Reviews page. "Mercedes GLE 500e plug-in hybrid (2015-2018)": www.carbuyer.co.uk/reviews/mercedes/gle/hybrid/review

Petrol SUV owners face tax rise to boost feeble electric car sales

Paton's article acknowledged that the reported overall increase in CO_2 emissions from new cars in recent years was at least partly attributable to the rise in *large*-SUV sales. He also explained that on April 1st. changes to Vehicle Excise Duty (VED) – often known as road tax – had been introduced which would penalize SUV ownership and incentivize electric-car ownership. By switching to the use of World Harmonised Light Vehicle Test Procedure (WLTP) measurements for CO_2 emissions, some loopholes from the previous system have been closed. Owners of certain SUVs with high CO_2 emissions, such as the Mercedes GLE 330d, will now have to pay a £750 premium in excess of the current annual charge. This article contained a list showing the maximum annual increase for a range of cars. Included in the list were the Jaguar F-Pace (£960), the VW Tiguan (£960), and the Kia Sportage. It also said that, according to AutoTrader magazine, owners of certain models of the Audi Q5 TDI will pay £1,815, an increase of £1,285. The way in which the article was written made me think that at long last some SUV owners might have financial cause for a rethink; and it seemed to have been a bold move by the government.

Sadly, I wasn't able to substantiate the figures provided in the article. Having downloaded and analysed the DVLA rates of road tax for myself, I was only able to conclude that what I'd read was actually somewhat misleading. No one was suddenly going to have found that, on April 1st 2020, the road tax for the car they drove had rocketed! The real story is that back in 2017 there was a major restructuring of VED which applied to vehicles registered on or after April 1st. the same year. This meant that vehicles with high CO_2 emissions would begin attracting a significantly higher first-year tax, one that currently increases to more than £2,000 for those with emissions over 255 g/km. The charge, however, *only* relates to new vehicles for their first year on the road. After year one, most petrol and diesel cars will attract a tax which is now £150 per year; considerably less than the graduated annual amount that still applies for many who have cars which were registered *before* April 1st 2017 and are in band F or above (i.e.

CO_2 readings in excess of 140 g/km). The re-structuring also targeted cars with a list price exceeding £40k by imposing an extra flat-rate premium for the five subsequent tax years after the WLTP-based first-year charge. This premium is currently £325, making the total annual road tax £475 for these five subsequent years. Given that the main structural changes themselves are now in their third year, the only people who were likely to have been caught out by the 2020 changes were those preparing to buy certain vehicles – including certain SUVs – whose new WLTP emissions rating edged them up into a higher class band. This would have resulted in a significant difference between the old first-year VED charge prior to April 1st., and the new WLTP-based first-year VED charge on or after it.

For those SUV drivers who had no intention of buying a new car, little changed on April 1st. 2020 to make them reconsider their position. In fact, if they bought their vehicle after April 1st 2017 and had therefore already absorbed the high first-year tax, then, provided their SUV didn't have a list price of more than £40k, many of them would have been – and still are – paying significantly less VED each year – £150 – than those driving exactly the same model who bought it on or before March 31st. 2017. *And if all that doesn't put your head in a spin, then nothing will.* Paton's article was a salutary illustration for me of just how careful we all need to be about not jumping onto issue bandwagons as a result of what we read in the press, even from a supposedly reputable newspaper such as The Times. Nonetheless, I'm grateful to the report for pointing me towards a clearer understanding of the incentives which have been introduced in favour of choosing an EV when buying a new car. EVs are now exempt from any VED – even the £325 annual premium on those costing more than £40k. In other words, the road tax for EV owners is zero. Taken together with the re-structured VED payments for a non-electric car, the government's hope is that car buyers will make the "clean" choice; that they will, for example, buy a Jaguar I-Pace SUV rather than a Jaguar F-Pace SUV.

An F-Pace will typically attract an initial year's road tax of £1,305, with five subsequent premium payments of £475. Assuming the vehicle is kept for the full six years, the VED liability will be £3,680 in total. Considering that showroom prices for the F-Pace are typically between £40k and £50k, I wonder if the amount of VED will be punitive enough to make someone consider buying a £65k zero-tax electric I-Pace instead? I somehow doubt it. But will the fuel savings make up the vital difference? If 5,320 miles worth of charging is done from home on an economy tariff of 12p per kWh, and 2,280 miles worth of charging is done from a roadside charging point at 30p per kWh, then, at 365 Watt hours per mile, the I-Pace will cost its owner about £482 over its annual 7,600 miles.[1] This contrasts with the £986 annual cost of running a diesel F-Pace at 42 mpg over the same distance – assuming current prices of about £5.45 per gallon. We can therefore calculate an additional saving of £3,024 over the six years. Whether or not the total saving of about £6.7k (£6,704) is enough, *in itself*, to tip the balance in favour of the electric I-Pace is very hard to call. If buyers expect filling station fuel prices to rise significantly in the coming years, this will add to the overall EV incentive of course; but the cost of installing charging equipment at home, or the practicalities of doing so (especially for many urban residents), is another weight to be placed on the opposite side of the scales.

I used the example of high-emissions and high-priced vehicles in the example I've just outlined: the Jaguar F-Pace and I-Pace. Had I chosen a Nissan Qashqai and the all-electric Peugeot e-2008 – a possible SUV alternative – as an example, then the figures seem to look even less persuasive so far as VED is concerned. First year VED on the Qashqai will be up to £215, with subsequent years being £150 indefinitely – disregarding any inflationary increases or any resulting from policy changes. Over six years, then, VED charges for the Qashqai are likely to be in the region of £965 more than for the zero-rated Peugeot e-2008, which is typically some £4k more expensive in the showroom. I wouldn't have thought that the tax saving would be enough to make much of a difference. Fuel-cost saving over the six years will be less than it was between the two

---

[1] Once again, the UK average, per car, is being used.

Jaguars given that the Qashqai in table 1 has a fuel economy of over 50 mpg; but it will still be somewhere in the region of £2,700. So it's the fuel-cost saving, if anything, that is likely to be the deciding factor in the choice between the two rather than road-tax saving. Without further insight into the influences on car-buying decisions, I have no real way of really knowing the extent to which the current VED structure will influence a switch to electric. My inclination is to think not very much; but that might just be me being a pessimistic wet rag. Perhaps the best that can be said is that the steeply graduated CO_2-related first-year charge may deter some people spending more than they can comfortably afford on a high-emission, high-VED non-electric SUV.

Even if the VED changes aren't yet either a sufficient stick or carrot to trigger a transitional stampede, they are no doubt another significant nudge in the direction that we're all being taken: the phased withdrawal of conventional diesel and petrol cars. Increased range and reduced showroom prices of EVs are also beginning to have a significant effect, which extends to SUVs. Those with a preference for Mercedes can now buy an EQC SUV with a range of 225 miles or more on a single charge, and those preferring Jaguar can buy the above mentioned I-Pace SUV with a range upwards of 230 miles. With the MG ZS also being available from £22,495, the electric SUV market is opening up, especially when the changes to VED and significantly cheaper fuel-related running costs are taken into consideration. Those who have previously avoided buying SUVs due to environmental considerations may now be starting to have a rethink. Some, perhaps many, may now feel that in the brave new electric world they can be allowed to indulge a previously supressed SUV passion with ethical impunity. The mantra of zero emissions will make it hard to carry on claiming that SUVs are an environmental menace. But before they are given their green-as-green-can-be certificate of merit, it needs to be remembered that whilst EVs are emission free at the point of use they are still only as "clean" as both the electricity which is used to charge their batteries and also the materials used in their construction. Consequently, their efficiency continues to be of importance! Two ways in which efficiency can be measured are by the Watt hours per mile (Wh/mi) and mpg equivalence.[1]

Vehicle Name	List Price (£)	Battery Rating (kWh)	Range (mi)	Efficiency (Wh/mi)	Fuel equivalent (mpg)
Seat Mii	19,800	32.3	125	255	202
MG ZS EV	22,495	44.5	140	315	149
Mini-e	24,900	28.9	115	250	204
Mazda MX 30 (concept)[2]	27,495	32	110	290	157
VW e-Golf	28,075	32	120	265	181
Peugeot e-2008	28,650	47.5	170	275	164
Nissan Leaf e+	33,295	56	205	270	173
VW ID.4 (concept)	37,000	77	260	295	163
Tesla Model 3	51,490	72.5	285	250	194
Audi Q4 e-tron	52,500	77	245	310	147
BMW i4 (concept)	55,000	80	275	290	189
Jaguar I-Pace	64,495	84.7	230	365	140
Mercedes EQC 400	65,640	80	225	355	131
Audi e-tron Sportback 55	79,185	86.5	235	365	130
Tesla Model S	82,190	95	325	290	161
Porsche Taycan 4S	83,365	71	230	305	144

Table 5: Sixteen EVs ordered by price. Data taken from the Electric Vehicle Database
(SUVs shaded yellow; concept vehicles are not yet in full production)

---

[1] It isn't entirely accurate to describe these indicators as measurements of efficiency. Strictly speaking, efficiency should be measured as a relationship between energy input and energy output: how well does any machine perform in converting one unit of energy input into output energy. But as we're interested in determining how "greedy" a particular vehicle is in its use of a scarce resource, these indicators can be used as a measurement of comparative performance.
[2] Some of the vehicles aren't yet available to order; they are therefore marked as "concept"

Taking information from the online Electric Vehicle Database,[1] I have compiled a small database of my own with relevant information for eight SUVs and eight GEN-Vs. I chose these particular cars as a selective representation across both the model and price range, and no information whatsoever relating to their performance was taken into consideration.

Table 5 above is ordered by price. When I re-ordered the data on the basis of efficiency (Wh/km), it became clear that the SUVs generally performed worse. Table 6 below clearly shows that there is a greater weighting of SUVs in the bottom – less efficient – half of the table. From the eight least efficient vehicles, six of them are SUVs. A similar finding resulted from organising the table according to fuel equivalence: Table 7 below.

In order to achieve a greater equivalence of comparison, I split the table into two: the eight cheapest vehicles and the eight most expensive – £19,800 (Seat Mii) to £37,000 (VW ID.4) and £51,490 (Tesla Model 3) to £79,185 (Audi e-tron Sportback 55). I then, once again, re-ordered each group of eight by efficiency (Wh/mi). The result is given as Table 8 below, which clearly shows the inefficiency of SUVs in comparison to their price-group peers. I repeated the exercise using mpg equivalence as the indicator of efficiency (table 9 below). The results are very nearly identical.

Vehicle Name	List Price (£)	Battery Rating (kWh)	Range (Mi)	Efficiency (Wh/mi)	Fuel equivalent (mpg)
Mini-e	24,900	28.9	115	250	204
Tesla Model 3	51,490	72.5	285	250	194
Seat Mii	19,800	32.3	125	255	202
VW e-Golf	28,075	32	120	265	181
Nissan Leaf e+	33,295	56	205	270	173
Peugeot e-2008	28,650	47.5	170	275	164
Mazda MX 30 (concept)	27,495	32	110	290	157
BMW i4 (concept)	55,000	80	275	290	189

(continued)

[1] Electric Vehicle Database: https://ev-database.uk

(continued)

Vehicle Name	List Price (£)	Battery Rating (kWh)	Range (Mi)	Efficiency (Wh/mi)	Fuel equivalent (mpg)
Tesla Model S	82,190	95	325	290	161
VW ID.4 (concept)	37,000	77	260	295	163
Porsche Taycan 4S	83,365	71	230	305	144
Audi Q4 e-tron	52,500	77	245	310	147
MG ZS EV	22,495	44.5	140	315	149
Mercedes EQC 400	65,640	80	225	355	131
Jaguar I-Pace	64,495	84.7	230	365	140
Audi e-tron Sportback 55	79,185	86.5	235	365	130

Table 6: Sixteen EVs ordered by efficiency (Wh/mi).

Vehicle Name	List Price (£)	Battery Rating (kWh)	Range (Mi)	Efficiency (Wh/mi)	Fuel equivalent (mpg)
Mini-e	24,900	28.9	115	250	204
Seat Mii	19,800	32.3	125	255	202
Tesla Model 3	51,490	72.5	285	250	194
BMW i4 (concept)	55,000	80	275	290	189
VW e-Golf	28,075	32	120	265	181
Nissan Leaf e+	33,295	56	205	270	173
Peugeot e-2008	28,650	47.5	170	275	164
VW ID.4 (concept)	37,000	77	260	295	163
Tesla Model S	82,190	95	325	290	161
Mazda MX 30 (concept)	27,495	32	110	290	157
MG ZS EV	22,495	44.5	140	315	149
Audi Q4 e-tron	52,500	77	245	310	147
Porsche Taycan 4S	83,365	71	230	305	144
Jaguar I-Pace	64,495	84.7	230	365	140
Mercedes EQC 400	65,640	80	225	355	131
Audi e-tron Sportback 55	79,185	86.5	235	365	130

Table 7: Sixteen EVs ordered by efficiency (Fuel Equivalent mpg)

Vehicle Name	List Price (£)	Battery Rating (kWh)	Range (Mi)	Efficiency (Wh/mi)	Fuel equivalent (mpg)
Mini-e	24,900	28.9	115	250	204
Seat Mii	19,800	32.3	125	255	202
VW e-Golf	28,075	32	120	265	181

(continued)

(continued)

Vehicle Name	List Price (£)	Battery Rating (kWh)	Range (Mi)	Efficiency (Wh/mi)	Fuel equivalent (mpg)
Nissan Leaf e+	33,295	56	205	270	173
Peugeot e-2008	28,650	47.5	170	275	164
Mazda MX 30 (concept)	27,495	32	110	290	157
VW ID.4 (concept)	37,000	77	260	295	163
MG ZS EV	22,495	44.5	140	315	149

Vehicle Name	List Price (£)	Battery Rating (kWh)	Range (Mi)	Efficiency (Wh/mi)	Fuel equivalent (mpg)
Tesla Model 3	51,490	72.5	285	250	194
BMW i4 (concept)	55,000	80	275	290	189
Tesla Model S	82,190	95	325	290	161
Porsche Taycan 4S	83,365	71	230	305	144
Audi Q4 e-tron	52,500	77	245	310	147
Mercedes EQC 400	65,640	80	225	355	131
Jaguar I-Pace	64,495	84.7	230	365	140
Audi e-tron Sportback 55	79,185	86.5	235	365	130

Table 8: Sixteen EVs grouped by price and then arranged by efficiency (Wh/mi)

Vehicle Name	List Price (£)	Battery Rating (kWh)	Range (Mi)	Efficiency (Wh/mi)	Fuel equivalent (mpg)
Mini-e	24,900	28.9	115	250	204
Seat Mii	19,800	32.3	125	255	202
VW e-Golf	28,075	32	120	265	181
Nissan Leaf e+	33,295	56	205	270	173
Peugeot e-2008	28,650	47.5	170	275	164
VW ID.4 (concept)	37,000	77	260	295	163
Mazda MX 30 (concept)	27,495	32	110	290	157
MG ZS EV	22,495	44.5	140	315	149

Vehicle Name	List Price (£)	Battery Rating (kWh)	Range (Mi)	Efficiency (Wh/mi)	Fuel equivalent (mpg)
Tesla Model 3	51,490	72.5	285	250	194
BMW i4 (concept)	55,000	80	275	290	189
Tesla Model S	82,190	95	325	290	161
Audi Q4 e-tron	52,500	77	245	310	147
Porsche Taycan 4S	83,365	71	230	305	144
Jaguar I-Pace	64,495	84.7	230	365	140
Mercedes EQC 400	65,640	80	225	355	131
Audi e-tron Sportback 55	79,185	86.5	235	365	130

Table 9: Sixteen EVs grouped by price and then arranged by efficiency (Fuel Equivalent mpg).

The intention at the outset of my research had been to illustrate the environmental irresponsibility of the growing SUV craze which we've witnessed throughout the first twenty years of the 21st century; years when the internal combustion engine remained the predominant source of motor vehicle power. In the previous chapters I've described and illustrated my fundamental dislike of SUVs and have gone on to substantiate my claim that in spite of engine-efficiency improvements they continue to be environmentally harmful. I believe that I've built a robust environmental case against SUVs based on their excessive CO_2 emissions and fuel inefficiency. Further still, taken together as a vehicle category, not only does their size mark them out as loud and aggressive but it also inevitably requires additional resources in their manufacture compared to smaller saloon or hatchback alternatives. By definition, the same size-and-shape-related arguments apply to SUVs powered by electricity. On these grounds alone my objections remain in place. And having demonstrated the comparative inefficiency of battery powered SUVs such as the Jaguar I-Pace compared to battery powered GEN-Vs such as the Tesla Model 3 (see table 9), I now need to discuss why this is important.

Even if our electricity came from entirely renewable sources such as the wind, the sun and the oceans and was therefore emission free at the point of generation, it would still remain true that harmful emissions are released and precious resources used in the construction of the requisite generating plant.[1] We should also be mindful of the additional resources which the electricity companies and the National Grid will use in order to create a distribution system that gets the electricity to the right places at the right time; an issue which is by no means inconsiderable given the struc-

---

[1] By way of illustration: – a wind turbine's carbon debt is calculated from a range of processes and materials which includes: cement and mineral quarrying to produce concrete for the foundations; steel to fabricate the towers; copper for generator windings and electric cables; fibre resin to manufacture the blades; transportation of components to wind farm sites (often remote), and access-track construction at the sites. It can take between nine months and several years of emission-free generation before the carbon dept is "repaid".

tural investment which will need to be made. The greater the demand for electricity, the more generating plant is needed and the more "upstream" emissions and resource depletion will result from its construction. It's a simple case of joining up the dots backwards if you like, and the dots are very much there to be joined; dots which run from the *comparative* inefficiency of the electric SUV to, for example, the mining of the cadmium, germanium, selenium and other metals needed for the production of solar panels in the clean-electricity scenario, or the continued reliance on natural gas in the dirty-electricity scenario. It's very similar to the line of dots that runs from the increased use of fuel in gas-guzzling vehicles to the finite supply of fossil fuels, albeit with a different start and end point: the increased Watt-hour mileage of a battery powered SUV leading to the increased use of those resources required to build and support an augmented electrical-supply system. And another issue that needs to be considered is the mining of cobalt for the production of EV batteries. Organisations such as Amnesty International have raised ethical concerns about the operation of cobalt mines in places such as the Democratic Republic of Congo.[1] Intensely important though this issue is, a more detailed examination of it belongs to others lest I deviate too far from my specific topic: the SUV craze and its environmental ramifications.

We don't yet live in the utopian world of 100% renewable electrical energy, far from it. So although the new generation of electric vehicles are emission-free at the point of use, they are far from emission-free at the point of the electricity generation needed for battery charging. It still remains true, therefore, that electric SUVs with their less efficient characteristics will generally be responsible for more global warming emissions than similar EVs which could have been bought instead. I would therefore like,

---

[1] World Economic Forum website. Industry agenda. "The dirty secret of electric vehicles." Douglas Broom: www.weforum.org/agenda/2019/03/the-dirty-secret-of-electric-vehicles

very briefly, to look at vehicle choice within the context of UK electricity generation.

Being perfectly honest with the facts as I understand them, I need to agree that my criticisms of SUVs become far less cogent once set within the context of EV-related electricity-generation emissions and our national global warming targets; and they continue weakening as we make further progress to meeting those targets with the use of clean generating facilities. Let me add some statistical substance to this. In 2019, taken over the whole year, renewable sources of electricity generation accounted for 33% of the total.[1] Further still, the group of generating sources classified by the Department for Business, Energy and Industrial Strategy (BEIS) as being "low carbon" accounted for 52.6% of the total. What is of concern to us in these figures is not so much any discussion of what counts as being "renewable" or "low carbon" as what it all means for the amount of CO_2 being emitted for each unit of electricity generated. This is helpfully provided for us by BEIS in the form of a measurement known as the "Grid Carbon Factor" (GCF). From a report published in April 2019 entitled "Updated Energy and Emissions Projections: 2018" we discover that the GCF in 2020 is expected to be 136 gCO_2e/kWh.[2] If that looks a little daunting, allow me to unravel it a bit. For each kilowatt hour (kWh) of electricity generated (the amount of electricity needed to power a 1kW household appliance such as small fan heater for an hour), 136 grams of global warming emissions, measured in equivalence to carbon dioxide (gCO_2e), will be produced. The lower the GCF is, the lower will be electricity-generation's contribution to global warming. Are you still with me? I hope so. I would just like us to remember one more number: **108**. This is the projected GCF (in gCO_2e/kWh) for

---

[1] Digest of UK Energy Statistics. Dukes 2019 Chapter 6. Renewable sources of energy: www.gov.uk/government/statistics/renewable-sources-of-energy-chapter-6-digest-of-united-kingdom-energy-statistics-dukes
[2] Gov.uk: www.gov.uk/government/publications/updated-energy-and-emissions-projections-2018

2025. The lower GCF figure – compared to the 2020 one – reflects the expected increase renewable and low-carbon generation will make to the total UK electricity supply.

Before pulling everything together, we need to remind ourselves from chapter four how important it is according to the Committee for Climate Change that every sector of our economy and society steps up its effort to help achieve the legally binding goal of net-zero greenhouse gas emissions by 2050. With this in mind, how do Sport Utility Electric Vehicles (SU-EVs) compare to General Electric Vehicles (GEN-EVs)? The average efficiency of the eight SU-EVs in table 5 worked out to be 321.25 Wh/mi.[1] Based on the UK car average of 7,600 miles per year, each vehicle will use 2,441.5 kWh of electricity. We can use the current GCF of 136 to establish that each car will therefore be responsible for generating just over 332 kg of CO_2e each year. By contrast, using the same methodology, the GEN-EVs will each be responsible for about 281 kg of CO_2e; 51 kg less.

Fifty-one kilograms of a gas might sound quite a lot; but in the big scheme of greenhouse gas emissions it becomes virtually insignificant – the proverbial drop in the ocean. It only remains of significance to those who want to take complete personal responsibility for global warming; to those who feel the burden of fighting climate change hangs heavily on their shoulders and want to do everything within their power to make a difference. From a personal don't-like-SUVs point of view, it would have been better for my case if these calculations had painted a more convincing picture; but they don't. Even the figures for emissions resulting from "collective" vehicle ownership aren't anything to write home about.

I made another of my economist's assumptions, that ownership of SU-EVs might grow at an annualized average of between ten and

---

[1]   This is a "simple" average. There isn't enough information yet available concerning registered numbers to produce a weighted average.

fifteen thousand to reach 50,000 by 2025. By the end of this year, on the basis of my assumptions, there will by 120,000 SU-EVs on the UK roads. Remember that by 2025, according to BEIS predictions, the Grid Carbon Factor will have fallen from to 136 to 108, which means the disparity between CO_2 emissions attributable to SU-EVs and GEN-EVs will have fallen further to just over 40 kg/yr.[1] Taken collectively, the 120,000 SU-EVs on our roads will be responsible for releasing an *extra* 4,863,240 kg of greenhouse gas emissions each year – measured in equivalence to CO_2 – compared to the amount for which the same number of GEN-EVs will be responsible. Holy Moses! That sounds like a vast amount; and in one sense it is: it's equivalent to the annual emissions from heating about 1,800 average UK homes. When compared to our national emissions targets, however, it only just about registers on the radar of statistical relevance: it's precisely 0.0324% of the annual 15 $MtCO_2$ reduction that the UK needs to make.

Perhaps we can look at it all one last way before bringing matters to a close. Firstly, we need to remind ourselves from Chapter four that the household heating carbon footprint in the UK is currently about 2,700 kg of CO_2 annually. I myself will almost certainly have the same Baxi boiler in 2025 as I presently have; so I don't expect this aspect of my carbon footprint to change much. This means that if, come 2025, I should decide to buy an SU-EV rather than a GEN-EV (almost unthinkable, of course, but please bear with me), I shall be responsible for additional emissions – 40 kg/yr – which are equivalent to about 1.5% of my home's heating carbon footprint. If nothing else, it's just about of statistical relevance; and I would always hope to reduce my overall carbon footprint rather than increase it. That said, I would be getting dangerously close to unwelcome environmental puritanism if I expected everyone else to have such overdeveloped scruples.

---

[1] 40.527 kg/yr.

The picture I've presented of EVs in general may seem to be prettier than the one you've read about; the one which takes into account the carbon footprint of battery production and which therefore reduces the overall benefit of going electric. The CO_2 savings derived from driving an EV are, it's true, partly offset by the heavy CO_2 "cost" of the batteries. Shouldn't I be including this in the same way I included the upstream cost of fossil fuel extraction and refining in relation to GEN-Vs and SUVs? The difference in our EV scenario is that the upstream CO_2 costs – primarily from battery production – are fixed per vehicle; they aren't being continuously added to whilst the vehicle is driven. As such, they remain a constant irrespective of whether it's an SU-EV that's being driven or a GEN-EV. It remains true that there *will* be marginal battery-size-related upstream-emissions differences between the two types of vehicles; and whilst I myself think that these are important enough to care about, I once again recognize the danger of environmental zealotry should I try to accommodate marginality of this order.

There can be little doubt that *any* EV driven on UK roads is considerably more carbon friendly than its fossil fuel relatives even after battery production has been accounted for. Transport & Environment, the European institute that I've already referred to several times, have produced an online tool that will enable Europeans to determine exactly how "clean" their EV is on the basis of where it's being driven and where the battery has been manufactured.[1] I've reproduced one of their illustrations below. It's a handy snapshot of an EV's environmental performance.

---

[1] Transport & Environment website. "How clean are electric cars?": www.transportenvironment.org/what-we-do/electric-cars/how-clean-are-electric-cars

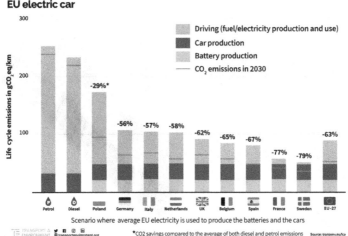

Today petrol and diesel cars emit almost 3 times more CO_2 than the average EU electric car

Electric Vehicle performance from Transport and Environment website: "How clean are electric cars?"

It would be wrong of me not to agree that owners of SU-EVs being driven on UK roads can hardly be called climate criminals, especially when their motoring carbon footprint is compared to that of someone who owns a diesel car – such as myself. And I haven't even yet drawn attention to the fact that many people will be charging their vehicles overnight at home. As such, on account of the input from onshore and offshore wind (which is typically greater throughout the night-time), the mix of electricity from renewable sources may well be higher than the annualized average. In consequence, then, of a lower overnight GCF, the amount of CO_2 emissions attributable to EVs is likely to be even lower than the figures I've used in the calculations of previous paragraphs.

In 2018, onshore wind contributed 27.5% to the renewable electricity total, and offshore wind 24.3%: 51.8% in total.[1] The

---

[1] Digest of UK Energy Statistics. Dukes 2019 Chapter 6. "Renewable sources of energy": www.gov.uk/government/statistics/renewable-sources-of-energy-chapter-6-digest-of-united-kingdom-energy-statistics-dukes

proportion will have increased by the year 2025 (as reflected in the lower GCF of 108), the year when I have assumed ownership of SU-EVs may have reached 120,000. If those driving these electric SUVs are able to do so with a relatively clear environmental conscience, then I would respectfully ask them to remember that in large measure they owe their guilt-free driving experience to all those wind turbines which I suspect many of them have cursed for being an invasion of the countryside – and scarcely able to boil a kettle according to one of their most vocal opponents, the late David Bellamy. Ten years or so ago when I threw my weight behind campaigns to build more onshore wind farms, I encountered the most vociferous opposition of all from those self-appointed countryside guardians who, if I may categorize them in a way which is probably unfair, were most likely to have been members of the Green-Wellies-and-Range-Rover elites. Back in 2010, the GCF was 485 gCO_2e/kWh[1], so the disparity between SU-EVs and GEN-EVs would have been 182 kg of CO_2 annually rather than the 40 kg projected for 2025.

Consider the following comparison as well, and please be tolerant of yet more assumptions and imaginings. Firstly, we need to suppose that both the Jaguar F-Pace SUV and I-Pace SU-EV had been in production back in 2010. We then need to suppose that an imaginary SUV driver – conjured up for the illustration – had driven an F-Pace with tailgate CO_2 emissions of 166 g/km over the 7,600 annual miles with which we've become familiar.[2] During the course of a year, he or she would have been responsible for 2,030 kg of CO_2 emissions. Supposing, on the other hand, that our imaginary person had been driving an I-Pace, then he or she would then have been responsible for 1,345 kg of emissions; only 685 kg less than from the non-electric sibling. Fast forward to 2020, with the current GCF of 136, and the comparable figure for

---

[1] Reported by the then Department of Energy and Climate Change in its "Conversion Factors 2010" document.

[2] Please remember, in case this distance seems low, that it's the average annual amount per car, not per person.

annual emissions attributable to the recently manufactured I-Pace is a meagre 377 kg of CO_2, a massive 1,653 kg less than the F-Pace – which would continue belching out the same annual amount. This clearly illustrates how the advent of "clean" driving with electric vehicles is directly related to the progress which has been made in renewable electricity generation, wind power in particular. The opposition I received during the years when I campaigned for various wind farms to be given planning permission was quite personal and sometimes extremely hurtful. In the end it became too much and I happily moved away from it all when it became necessary to care for my elderly parents. Thankfully, many of the wind farms I supported have now been built, and I smile to see their blades spinning joyfully in a display of mechanical ballet. I hope that they are properly appreciated by any of those who once opposed them but now find themselves able to drive an EV, maybe an SU-EV, with a reasonably clear environmental conscience. With that said, I shall try to ignore the ghosts of those unhappy years; phantoms who occasionally return to haunt my memories.

If the GCF continues the downward trajectory predicted by BEIS (and it will *have* to if the mandatory target of net-zero by 2050 is to be met), then any disparity between the carbon footprint of different kinds of electric vehicles will eventually become so marginal as to be virtually meaningless.[1] The only objections remaining to SU-EVs will be those I have already spoken of; those which relate to their appearance, the fact they inevitably use more of scarce resources in their manufacture than smaller vehicles, and their general statement of being bigger-and-better than the rest.

---

[1] What remains will be the additional carbon footprint of providing marginally more generating capacity (e.g. extra wind turbines) to meet the increased charging needs of SU-EVs compared to GEN-EVs; and also the additional carbon footprint of manufacturing larger vehicles.

Chapter Eight

THE FINAL WORD

This final chapter was largely completed by the end of May 2020. My many corrections and revisions to the book have taken me several more months, but I have left these final words as close to the original ones as possible.

Based on current evidence, it's hard to believe that enough people will be willing to make the tough choices necessary for the UK to meet its 2050 net-zero emissions target; even harder to think that the necessary global action will be taken. The number of SUVs on our roads has yet to peak, and their numbers will be augmented by the next generation of SU-EVs. Whether or not the pleasure to be derived from owning and driving one of these buses is compensation for living in world whose natural wildlife, beauty and diversity is increasingly destroyed by a hostile climate is hard to know. I suspect that the answer for those who drive them is yes. Sadly, and regrettably, I don't think that those who have bought into the current SUV madness can possibly care about what's being lost, only what's important to them.

The backdrop to this project has been that I don't have much hope we'll be successful in our mission to bring global greenhouse gas emissions under control given how many people are making decisions which I believe to be gratuitously selfish: selfish in the context of the responsibility we all share to "make a difference". I've therefore elaborated on how I feel about the phenomenal rise of SUVs and afforded some factual substance to *why* I feel this way. I don't suppose for one minute that many people are going to change their behaviour as a result of reading my little book; although, supposing that there are any SUV owners who've read it through to here, I hope I've given plenty to think about, or even laugh at in places – at my own foibles if nothing else.

That may all sound rather hopeless and pessimistic. But it's also true that I've seen this project through to the end because I've believed it to be the best contribution I can make. As such, I've been guided by that wonderful Chinese proverb, the inspiration for Amnesty International's logo: *it's better to light a candle than curse the darkness.* This book is one of my little candles! There will some SUV owners who will say, of course, that they didn't know; they had no idea that indulging their lust for vehicle superiority was so environmentally selfish. Maybe not. But I don't accept *not knowing* as an excuse for *not finding out.* It's often the case that the things we don't know about are the very same things that we don't *want* to know about. It would be more honest, I think, for people to say that they didn't care rather than didn't know.

As we begin to move away from our lockdown here in the UK, maybe something has changed as a result of what we've been through together which will make us start caring a bit more about the world we live in once again. For many, the end of the ordeal probably can't come soon enough. My heart genuinely goes out to those far less fortunate than Jeanne and I have been so far; those whose lives have been devastated by ruin or loss. In my own small way I too am suffering. I'm still experiencing complications subsequent to the prostate cancer surgery I had last year. The remedial surgery I had hoped to have was put on hold, and still is. Worse still are the complications that have resulted from the knee replacement surgery I had later in the year. Nine months on and I now have to walk using crutches; and my knee is supported with several layers of taping, dressing and bracing. It's been established that I have torn and damaged tendons. But without further treatment I won't get any better, and I seem to be getting worse.

In spite of this, I know that I'm by no means alone in sensing a new "something" in the air, a new something which makes many hopeful of a better future.[1] There is a strange sense of peace as we try to find meaning, enjoyment and purpose in our changed lives. The once-busy city roads are still far quieter; and for those of us lucky enough to have gardens the birdsong seems much louder than normal. We are rediscovering things like the joy of taking things easy; making do with far far less than normal as many shops have been closed and we wanted to avoid queuing to get into those which weren't. Across the world, it feels as if nature is inhaling one huge cleansing breath; breathing in life-supporting air that is cleaner than we've known for decades. In Delhi, the Himalayan mountains can be seen one hundred miles away; for those under a certain age, this will be for the first time. It is indeed a Silent Spring; but not the one which Rachel Carson imagined. The voice of nature seems to be singing far louder now that the noise of mankind has been subdued, at least temporarily.

Will these changes persist in any way as we get back to normal? What will the new normal be like? Who can tell? Certainly not me! I can hope that something good comes from all this: I can and I will. Would it be cranky if I asked out loud whether or not nature has had some kind of guiding hand? Yes! It probably would be! And yet I can't help but wonder.

Without disrespect to those who have suffered badly, I confess to having enjoyed the enforced pause in quite a few ways – not all of course – and I hope it may have a lasting effect which is beneficial for the planet. Will the expansion of Heathrow airport or the HS2 project really be needed in our new world? How soon will it be before the volume of flights and demand for rail travel returns to what it was? I imagine that many people are going to re-evaluate their attitude to flying and travel in general, and for many different reasons. Our GDP will inevitable shrink; but no one really knows by how much. And maybe it won't be such a catastrophic event as

---

[1] Maybe, for myself, I'm confusing this with the newly gained hope that Luton Town can play their way out of the Championship relegation zone now that football is at long last back with us.

might be supposed. We're constantly being told that our economy must grow, grow, grow; and heaven help us if it doesn't. Will its contraction be as calamitous as we've been told for so long such a thing would be? And there I go again with my questions.

Thank you for reading this. I hope I'm wrong about it all. I hope that we'll collectively avert the devastation that will come from a climate spiralling out of control if and when feedback-effects start to kick in. Maybe mother nature herself will give us a helping hand to make the necessary changes. I hope that if I live to what they call a ripe old age and I'm still here to re-read this booklet in twenty or thirty years' time I'll chuckle at how wrong I was to be have been so pessimistic.[1]

---

[1] (See footnote 1 from previous page) The Hatters did it! It came right down to the last few minutes of the final behind-closed-doors Championship games. But we did it.

APPENDICES.

Explanations of methodology and arithmetical calculations

Appendix One. Use of Department for Transport (DfT) Data

Analysis

My raw data has been extracted from the Department for Transport (DfT) Vehicle Licensing statistics. www.gov.uk/government/collections/vehicles-statistics:

(1) Table VEH0160:
     Cars registered for the first time by make and model, Great Britain from 2001 Q1; also United Kingdom from 2014 Q3

(2) Table VEH0128:
     Licensed cars at the end of the quarter by generic model, Great Britain from 1994 Q4; also United Kingdom from 2014 Q4

As the data for the UK only goes back as far as 2014, I chose to use the data for GB – which is available back to 2001. Where this affects my analysis – i.e. comparing GB vehicle data with other data that relates to the whole of the UK – I have made acknowledgement in the text.

The UK registration details will invariably return larger numbers than the GB details owing to the inclusion of Northern Ireland. Total **GB** registrations in 2018, for example, were 2,341,505 compared to 2,731,434 for the **UK**. This isn't of great significance, however, as I have only been loosely concerned with total vehicle sales, per se. My main concern has been to identify *patterns* of registrations within a total, and it's of little importance whether this is a GB total or a UK total. Where necessary, I have drawn attention to the difference between UK and GB figures in the body of my text.

As the DfT data in table VEH0160 didn't give totals for each specific model of vehicle, I organized the data myself on the basis of the line descriptions given on each spreadsheet row. In the case of the Land Rover Discovery, for example, there were 141 rows, each with a different descriptor (e.g. DISCOVERY SPORT LANDMARK TD4 A; DISCOVERY HSE TD6 AUTO; DISCOVERY SPORT HSE SI4 AUTO).

I collated each of these 141-line listings as one model: **Land Rover Discovery**. In this way, I ended up with data for 482 different models of vehicle under the general listing of "cars".

The DfT spreadsheet data also included rows which, although populated, were labelled as "MISSING". These related to instances where it hadn't been possible to cross reference a specific vehicle line/trim with a manufacturer's code.

SUVs

I identified SUVs on the basis of their description by manufacturers. This includes all vehicles being promoted as being an SUV or a Crossover SUV. The list of all 157 SUVs is given below as table 1a.

Generic model	2019 Q4 GB	2018 Q4 GB
Electric		
JAGUAR I-PACE	4690	792
KIA NIRO EV	666	0
KIA SOUL EV	973	943
MERCEDES EQC CLASS	149	
Non-Electric		
ALFA ROMEO STELVIO	2371	1254
AUDI Q2	41969	26965

(continued)

(continued)

Generic model	2019 Q4 GB	2018 Q4 GB
AUDI Q3	103704	91465
AUDI Q5	81533	70680
AUDI Q7	43476	40329
AUDI Q8	2463	704
AUDI SQ2	837	
AUDI SQ5	10304	10061
AUDI SQ7	2227	2185
AUDI SQ8	120	
BENTLEY BENTAYGA	1902	1501
BMW X1	89762	77850
BMW X2	11397	4714
BMW X3	92742	79904
BMW X4	13147	9601
BMW X5	94933	91991
BMW X6	14424	14113
BMW X7	517	
CHEVROLET CAPTIVA	9231	9810
CHEVROLET TRAX	1546	1560
CITROEN C3 AIRCROSS	20222	10524
CITROEN C5 AIRCROSS	6664	21
DACIA DUSTER	54895	40477
DAIHATSU TERIOS	6196	6998
FIAT 500X	5390	1951
FORD ECOSPORT	85597	61644
FORD EDGE	8474	7728
FORD FIESTA ACTIVE	13105	4316
FORD FOCUS ACTIVE	5487	3
FORD KA ACTIVE	6012	1999
FORD KUGA	250839	212577
HONDA CRV	208769	217389
HONDA CR-V	9157	1333
HONDA HR-V	30637	27075
HYUNDAI SANTA	39726	41195
HYUNDAI SANTA FE		
HYUNDAI KONA	14836	7072
HYUNDAI TUCSON	109473	88649
INFINITI QX30	290	213

(continued)

(continued)

Generic model	2019 Q4 GB	2018 Q4 GB
INFINITI QX50	70	72
INFINITI QX70	411	421
ISUZU TROOPER	3501	4307
JAGUAR E-PACE	20834	10110
JAGUAR F-PACE	39570	30231
JEEP CHEROKEE	31560	35707
JEEP COMMANDER	982	1068
JEEP COMPASS	8283	5253
JEEP G-CHEROKEE	109	118
JEEP GRAND CHEROKEE	6241	6092
JEEP MODEL MISSING	603	576
JEEP PATRIOT	3674	3997
JEEP RENEGADE	23875	22379
JEEP WRANGLER	5944	5410
KIA NIRO	20251	11872
KIA SORENTO	42041	41830
KIA SOUL	22148	22102
KIA SPORTAGE	236624	208269
KIA STONIC	15166	6895
KIA XCEED	935	
LAMBORGHINI URUS	321	80
LAND ROVER 109	263	271
LAND ROVER 110	1301	1384
LAND ROVER 127	5	6
LAND ROVER 88	559	544
LAND ROVER 90	1065	1155
LAND ROVER DEFENDER	12768	13084
LAND ROVER DISCOVERY	253598	239892
LAND ROVER DISCO-Y		
LAND ROVER FREELANDER	152297	163046
LAND ROVER RANGE ROVER	391190	353567
LEXUS NX200	140	152
LEXUS NX300	20081	16110
LEXUS RX 350		
LEXUS RX 450		
LEXUS RX200	60	69

(continued)

(continued)

Generic model	2019 Q4 GB	2018 Q4 GB
LEXUS RX300	6913	7907
LEXUS RX350	1069	1130
LEXUS RX400	10050	10339
LEXUS RX450	19820	18278
LEXUS RXL450	894	416
LEXUS UX 250H	3360	
MASERATI LEVANTE	1908	1487
MAZDA CX3	36845	21264
MAZDA CX30	233	
MAZDA CX5	42609	41617
MAZDA CX7	2281	2475
MERCEDES AMG G, GLA, GLC, GLE, GLS	7094	5068
MERCEDES G CLASS	2066	1971
MERCEDES GL CLASS	2803	3016
MERCEDES GLA CLASS	67780	51367
MERCEDES GLC CLASS	61423	45652
MERCEDES GLE CLASS	18948	16939
MERCEDES GLS CLASS	2066	1868
MERCEDES ML CLASS	45575	50251
MG GS	2699	2358
MG ZS	3565	3296
MG HS	96	
MG XS	12197	5226
MINI COUNTRYMAN	97498	93672
MINI COUNTRYMAN COOPER		1393
MINI PACEMAN	9457	
MINI PACEMAN COOPER		9357
MITSUBISHI ASX	27882	26598
MITSUBISHI CHALLENGER	254	346
MITSUBISHI ECLIPSE CROSS	9661	5637
MITSUBISHI OUTLANDER	69497	62370
MITSUBISHI PAJERO	310	387
MITSUBISHI SHOGUN	40502	44794
NISSAN JUKE	272945	253853

(continued)

(continued)

Generic model	2019 Q4 GB	2018 Q4 GB
NISSAN QASHQAI	519523	476150
NISSAN X-TRAIL	101273	101666
PEUGEOT 2008	93356	81553
PEUGEOT 3008	122837	104889
PEUGEOT 4007	2044	2188
PEUGEOT 5008	27226	22068
PORSCHE CAYENNE	27804	25292
PORSCHE MACAN	22789	18353
RENAULT CAPTUR	127633	107753
RENAULT KOLEOS	4465	3611
RENAULT KADJAR	57544	46982
ROLLS ROYCE CULLINAN	172	26
SEAT ARONA	26642	12496
SEAT ATECA	30946	20763
SEAT TARRACO	4022	
SKODA KAROQ	27949	13626
SKODA KODIAQ	22121	13857
SKODA YETI	75193	75349
SSANGYONG KORANDO	6285	5660
SSANGYONG KYRON	480	598
SSANGYONG REXTON	3901	3976
SSANGYONG TIVOLI	5899	5164
SUBARU FORESTER	19480	19845
SUBARU XV	5512	4663
SUZUKI GRAND VITARA	263	269
SUZUKI JIMNY	26464	26911
SUZUKI SX4 S-CROSS	21520	19478
SUZUKI VITARA	87320	79799
TOYOTA C-HR	48211	31802
TOYOTA LANDCRUISER	23747	24906
TOYOTA RAV4	130912	129717
VAUXHALL ANTARA	23879	24411
VAUXHALL CROSSLAND X	29675	14395
VAUXHALL FRONTERA	2358	3201
VAUXHALL GRANDLAND X	36518	15781
VAUXHALL MOKKA	211795	190739
VOLKSWAGEN T-CROSS	6607	

(continued)

(continued)

Generic model	2019 Q4 GB	2018 Q4 GB
VOLKSWAGEN TIGUAN	192594	159698
VOLKSWAGEN TOUAREG	38478	36981
VOLKSWAGEN T-ROC	35722	15598
VOLVO XC40	21282	6535
VOLVO XC60	95670	85175
VOLVO XC70	18932	19403
VOLVO XC90	68829	63854
Total non-electric SUVs	6147016	5377433
Total SUVs	6153494	5379168

Table 1a: Licensed SUVs at Q4 of 2018 and 2019 by generic model

Make	Model [1]	2018 Q4 GB	2018 Q3 GB	2018 Q2 GB	2018 Q1 GB	2018 Total
NISSAN	QASHQAIA	8386	11473	12822	16607	49288
LAND ROVER	RANGE ROVER	11483	11970	11156	14497	49106
FORD	KUGA	7662	10302	8364	12628	38956
KIA	SPORTAGE	6613	9802	8113	10034	34562
VAUXHALL	MOKKA & MOKKA X	6030	7290	7635	10575	31530
VOLKSWAGEN	TIGUAN	7569	6018	8191	9106	30884
LAND ROVER	DISCOVERY	6066	6825	6193	8874	27958
HYUNDAI	TUCSON	3971	7943	6889	7513	26316
NISSAN	JUKE	4357	8146	4838	6686	24027
FORD	ECOSPORT	4989	5780	6076	5393	22238
RENAULT	CAPTUR	4133	5690	4588	6564	20975
MERCEDES	GLC range	3551	5863	5578	5811	20803
PEUGEOT	3008	3633	4664	5187	5848	19332
TOYOTA	C-HR	3620	5429	4212	5035	18296
MERCEDES	GLA Series	4769	4508	3134	4527	16938
VAUXHALL	GRANDLAND X	4046	5747	2887	3529	16209
PEUGEOT	2008	2903	4389	3659	5221	16172
VOLKSWAGEN	T-ROC	5200	3970	3713	2922	15805
BMW	X1	3039	2841	4509	4315	14704
AUDI	Q2	2505	2605	4848	4641	14599

Table 2a: Top twenty SUVs by 2018 registration totals.

Car registrations v. car sales

Car registration figures will not always be the same as car sales, as explained by Jim Holder writing in a 2016 Autocar magazine article.[1] The difference is essentially explained by car dealers registering vehicles before they have actually been sold, meaning that there could be a stock of unsold cars within the dealerships.

There are, however, no phantom car registrations; which means that the registration figures do, ultimately, represent a new car that has been registered and will end up being bought by a customer, even if there is a time lag between registration and sales.

For the purpose of my discussion, I have used the two terms "car registrations" and "car sales" more or less interchangeably.

---

[1] Autocar magazine. Opinion page. "Car Registrations v car sales": www. autocar.co.uk/opinion/industry/car-registrations-vs-car-sales

Appendix Two. Representative information for vehicle models

Calculation of averages

General methodology

Calculating average CO_2 emissions and mpg for a given model has been a challenge. There isn't, for example, one line of vehicle which is the Ford Fiesta. The DfT statistics, in fact, list 277 current or historical lines. To illustrate, I have produced a "2018 top-ten" list as table 3a.

Make	Model 1	2018 Q4 GB	2018 Q3 GB	2018 Q2 GB	2018 Q1 GB	2018 Total
FORD	FIESTA ZETEC	3715	3964	3701	7196	18576
FORD	FIESTA ZETEC TURBO	2576	4129	5001	6465	18171
FORD	FIESTA ST-LINE TURBO	2051	3171	4139	6168	15529
FORD	FIESTA TITANIUM TURBO	1994	3457	3594	5982	15027
FORD	FIESTA ST-LINE X TURBO	615	845	1627	719	3806
FORD	FIESTA TITANIUM TURBO AUTO	371	662	777	772	2582
FORD	FIESTA ZETEC TURBO AUTO	482	445	668	986	2581
FORD	FIESTA VIGNALE TURBO	336	481	409	428	1654
FORD	FIESTA ST-3 TURBO	804	583	75		1462
FORD	FIESTA TITANIUM X TURBO	243	292	438	458	1431

Table 3a: Example of DFT listings. Top-ten lines of Ford Fiesta registrations in 2018

When I cross referenced these models with vehicle specifications provided by, for instance, the BBC Top Gear online reviews, many of them had slightly different model descriptors. It became almost impossible, therefore, to ensure that I had identified the correct model line from information provided by the DFT. I also needed to decide how to incorporate the *specific* information for each model line when there were so many of them. For consistency, therefore, I decided to restrict my analysis to the top selling line for each model[1] – in this case the Fiesta Zetec – and use its data (e.g. CO_2 emissions and mpg) as representative of all the models. I recognize that this is

---

[1] The only exception – in order to accommodate the hybrid models – to this was the Toyota Yaris. See Appendix 3

prone to error, but because the methodology is being applied consistently for all ten SUVs and all ten GEN-Vs, then I believe the resulting averages are adequate for purposes of comparison.

Using this method, the Ford Fiesta Zetec (fitted with a 1.0 Ecoboost engine) was shown to have CO_2 emissions of 110 g/km. I compared this to the average CO_2 for all 88 models of Fiesta reviewed by BBC Top Gear,[1] which was 109.14 g/km. This confirmed my methodology to be sufficiently robust for the purpose of my analysis.

Given the way in which the DFT data is presented, I have necessarily had to sometimes make judgements about the model being referenced as this doesn't always neatly correspond to a manufacturer's description. I have taken considerable effort to ensure that my choices are representative.

Toyota Yaris methodology

The exception to the above was the Toyota Yaris. Given that a model with a hybrid engine (HEV) was the bestselling model (YARIS ICON TECH VVT-I HEV CVT), I was concerned that it would distort the data if I used these low emissions and high mpg as representative of the whole range. Throughout the entire Yaris model range, there is a mixture of vehicles fitted with hybrid and non-hybrid vehicles. I therefore worked out a weighted average of the top two selling models as shown in Table 3a. (The YARIS ICON TECH VVT-I is a non-hybrid model) as being representative

	CO_2 (g/km)	mpg	Nos
YARIS ICON TECH VVT-I HEV CVT	75	85.6	5542
YARIS ICON TECH VVT-I	116	55.4	4350
Total			9,892.00
Weighted Averages	93.03	72.32	

Table 4a: Weighted average data calculation for the Toyota Yaris

---

[1] BBC Top Gear website. Reviews: www.topgear.com/car-reviews/ford/fiesta/specs

In the above table, the weighted average for CO_2 emissions (93.03 g/km) is given by 75 x 5542/9892 + 111 x 4350/9892

Kerb weight information

Kerb Weight is far more uniform across the model range: i.e. there is less variation between the model lines as there is for emissions and mpg. The kerb weight shown in the tables, therefore, can be relied on as being representative

Appendix Three. Calculation of weighted averages for top-ten SUVs and GEN-Vs

Methodology

Vehicle	CO_2 (g/km)	mpg **	Kerb Weight (Kg)	Length (m)	Width (m)	List Price (£)	Euro NCAP Safety (%)				2018 "line" numbers	2018 "model" numbers
							A	B	C	D		
Ford Fiesta: 1.0 EcoBoost Zetec 5dr	110	58.9	1,163	4.04	1.94	16,515	87	84	64	60	18,576	90,225
Volkswagen Golf: 1.5 TSI EVO SE [Nav] 5dr	113	56.5	1,280	4.26	2.03	21,930	95	89	76	78	5,422	61,362
Vauxhall Corsa: 1.2 Energy 3dr [AC]	124	53.3	1,166	4.02	1.94	12,545	79	77	71	56	8,967	52,455
Ford Focus: 1.5 EcoBoost ST-Line 5dr	127	51.4	1,250	4.36	2.01	21,290	92	82	72	71	8,804	49,574
Volkswagen Polo: 1.0 TSI 95 SE 5dr	105	61.4	1,069	4.05	1.96	16,775	96	85	76	59	18,398	44,050
Mercedes-Benz A Class A180d: Sport Executive 5dr Auto	103	67.3	1,425	4.3	2.02	26,585	93	81	67	86	4,589	42,862
Mini Hatchback: 1.5 Cooper 5dr	109	60.1	1,145	3.98	1.93	16,615	79	73	66	56	17,447	40,005
Vauxhall Astra: 1.5 Turbo D 105 SRi 5dr	90	64.2	1,403	4.37	2.04	22,730	86	84	83	75	3,419	30,280
Mercedes C class: C220d AMG Line 4dr Auto	117	62.8	1,570	4.68	2.02	35,740	89	79	66	53	4,733	29,579

(continued)

139

(continued)

Vehicle	CO_2 (g/ km)	mpg **	Kerb Weight (Kg)	Length (m)	Width (m)	List Price (£)	Euro NCAP Safety (%)				2018 "line" numbers	2018 "model" numbers
							A	B	C	D		
Toyota Yaris: 1.5 VVT-i Icon Tech 5dr	93	72.3	975	3.95	1.9	16,145	89	81	60	86	10,992	28,388
Weighted Average (All)	111	60	1,231	Safety Average			89	82	70	68	Total	468,780
Weighted Average (Top 3)	115	57	1,199			Worst	A = Adult Occupant					
Weighted Average (Top 6)	114	58	1,218			Best	B = Child Occupant					
** mpg data relates to EC "combined cycle"						Highest	C = Vulnerable Road User					
						Lowest	D = Safety Assist					

Table 5a: Copy of table 1 showing data for top-ten GEN-Vs

I applied weighting to CO_2, mpg and Kerb Weight information so that, for example, the Ford Fiesta data with model registrations of 90,225 would be correctly represented in relation to the other models with fewer registrations.

The CO_2 weighted averages in the above table are based on the following formula:

A1 x B1/C + A2 x B2/C ... up to A10 x B10/C

Where A1, A2 etc are the CO_2 figures for Ford Fiesta, VW Golf etc.
Where B1, B2 etc are the 2018 "model" numbers for Ford Fiesta, VW Golf etc.
Where C = Total registration number for all 10 vehicles (468,780)

A similar methodology is used to arrive at weighted averages for MPG and Kerb Weight.

The process of calculation for SUV weighted averages is identical.

Appendix Four: Calculation of weighted averages for pickups.

Methodology

I chose, as explained in the text, to use data from the top-six pickups, which had 48,872 registrations in 2018; 96% of the annual total.

Vehicle	CO_2 (g/ km)	mpg **	Kerb Weight (kg)	Length (m)	Width (m)	List Price (£)	Euro NCAP Safety (%)				2018 "model" numbers
	Average across range						A	B	C	D	
Ford Ranger	209	35.7	1917	5.36	2.16	33,404	96	86	81	71	15914
Mitsubishi L200	186	39.8	1790	5.28	1.81	25,050	81	84	76	64	9045
Nissan Navara	172	43.6	1991	5.33	2.08	31,360	79	78	78	68	9062
Toyota Hilux	189	39.1	1880	5.33	1.85	26,340	93	82	83	63	6814
Isuzu D-Max	183	40.4	1994	5.29	1.86	20,499	83	67	51	71	4748
VW Amarok	203	36.2	1880	5.25	1.95	36,991	86	64	47	57	3289
Weighted Average (All)	192	38.9	1901	Safety Average			86	77	69	66	48872

** mpg data relates to EC "combined cycle"		Worst	A = Adult Occupant
		Best	B = Child Occupant
		Highest	C = Vulnerable Road User
		Lowest	D = Safety Assist

Table 6a: Copy of Table 4 – calculation of weighted averages for pickups

Ford Ranger Example

Whereas the CO_2 and mpg data for SUVs and GEN-Vs was based on the bestselling line/trim of a given model, I was able to take a more detailed approach with pickups on account of the smaller line/trim range.

The information below illustrates my calculation methodology

Vehicle	CO_2 (g/km)	mpg	2018 Nos
FORD RANGER WILDTRAK 4X4 DCB TDCI A	221	33.60	10,992.00
FORD RANGER LIMITED 4X4 DCB TDCI A	184	40.40	4,922.00
Total			15,914.00
Weighted Average	209.56	35.70	

Table 7a: Weighted averages emissions and mpg for the Ford Ranger

For each model – e.g. the Ford Ranger – I took the total number of registrations for the top 2 selling lines; in this case:

(i)   **Ford Ranger 3.2 Duratorq TDCi 200PS Double Cab 4x4 Wildtrak 4dr Auto &**

(ii)   **Ford Ranger 3.2 Duratorq TDCi 200PS Double Cab 4x4 Wildtrak 4dr.**

For these two vehicles combined, 2018 registrations were 10,992

I then used information from either Top Gear or Autocar magazine to establish representative CO_2 and mpg data, taking a simple average if there was a significant variation between the two. In table 7a above this shows 221 g/km and 33.6 mpg

For the remaining registrations (4,922) I was able to look at the data supplied by BBC Top Gear or Autocar for the various model lines involved. I chose the *lowest* of the CO_2 readings and the *highest* MPG readings: 184 g/km and 40.4mpg in table 7a.

Next, I calculated a weighted average based on the model line numbers as a fraction of total model registrations: 209.56 g CO_2/km and 35.7 mpg in table 7a. These are the figures which were used as representative of the model in table 4 of the main text, copied as table 6a above.

Finally, I calculated a weighted average for all 6 vehicles using model numbers as a fraction of the 48,872 total registrations.

As explained in the main text, these 48,872 vehicles constitute 96% of the actual 2018 total (50,951) and I can therefore feel confident in taking my weighted averages as being representative of the whole.

Why the methodology results in an under-representation of SUV impact

On account of my methodology, if any bias is reflected in my calculations it will be to lower the final weighted averages for CO_2 and raise the mpg averages. As it is my intention to demonstrate how high the emissions from these vehicles are, and also to show how poor the fuel efficiency is, the bias will mean that I am understating rather than overstating the case. In other words, the situation is even worse than I am representing it to be on the basis of the data being used.

Mitsubishi L200, Nissan Navara and Toyota Hilux

For reference, tables 8a to 10a show the data used for 3 of the remaining pickup models.

Vehicle Model (DfT Descripton)	co₂ (g/km)	mpg	Nos
L200 BARBARIAN, TITAN & WARRIOR	186	39.80	8,241.00
L200 4LIFE DI-D	184	40.40	804.00
Total Model Registrations			9,045.00
Weighted Average	185.82	39.85	

Table 8a: Weighted average emissions and mpg for the Mitsubishi L200

Vehicle Model (DfT Descripton)	co₂ (g/km)	mpg	Nos
NAVARA TEKNA DCI AUTO & MANUAL	173	43.40	7,742.00
NAVARA CONNECTA MANUAL	167	44.90	1,320.00
Total Model Registrations			9,062.00
Weighted Average	172.13	43.62	

Table 9a: Weighted average emissions and mpg for the Nissan Navara

Vehicle Model (DfT Descripton)	co₂ (g/km)	mpg	Nos
TOYOTA HILUX ACTIVE AND INVINCIBLE	194	38.10	2,866.00
HILUX INVINCIBLE D-4D 4WDDCB A	185	39.80	3,948.00
Total Model Registrations			6,814.00
Weighted Average	188.79	39.08	

Table 10a: Weighted average emissions and mpg for the Toyota Hilux

A simplified version of the calculation process was used for the Isuzu D-Max and the VW Amorak on account of their comparatively low registration figures.

Kerb weight doesn't tend to vary significantly across the model lines. For the six vehicles in question, therefore, data relating to the best-selling line for each model was used.

INDEX

Lightning Source UK Ltd.
Milton Keynes UK
UKHW021111290421
382823UK00007B/86